I0426256

July 2012

REFUGEE RESETTLEMENT

Greater Consultation with Community Stakeholders Could Strengthen Program

G A O
Accountability ★ Integrity ★ Reliability

July 2012

REFUGEE RESETTLEMENT

Greater Consultation with Community Stakeholders Could Strengthen Program

Why GAO Did This Study

In fiscal year 2011, the United States admitted more than 56,000 refugees under its refugee resettlement program. Upon entry, a network of private, nonprofit voluntary agencies (voluntary agencies) selects the communities where refugees will live. The Department of State's PRM and the Department of Health and Human Services' ORR provide funding to help refugees settle in their communities and obtain employment and monitor implementation of the program. Congress has begun to reexamine the refugee resettlement program, and GAO was asked to examine (1) the factors resettlement agencies consider when determining where refugees are initially placed; (2) the effects refugees have on their communities; (3) how federal agencies ensure program effectiveness and integrity; and (4) what is known about the integration of refugees. GAO reviewed agency guidance, monitoring protocols, reports, and studies; conducted a literature review; reviewed and analyzed relevant federal and state laws and regulations; and met with federal and state officials, voluntary agency staff, and local stakeholders in eight selected communities.

What GAO Recommends

GAO makes several recommendations to the Secretaries of State and Health and Human Services to improve refugee assistance programs in the United States. HHS and State generally concurred with the recommendations and each identified efforts they have under way or plan to undertake to address them.

View GAO-12-729. For more information, contact Kay Brown at (202) 512-7215 or brownke@gao.gov.

What GAO Found

Voluntary agencies consider various factors when determining where refugees will be placed, but few agencies we visited consulted relevant local stakeholders, which posed challenges for service providers. When deciding how many refugees to place in each community, some voluntary agencies prioritize local agency capacity, such as staffing levels, while others emphasize community capacity, such as housing availability. Although the Immigration and Nationality Act states that it is the intent of Congress for voluntary agencies to work closely with state and local stakeholders when making these decisions, the Department of State's Bureau of Population, Refugees, and Migration (PRM) offers limited guidance on how this should occur. Some communities GAO visited had developed formal processes for obtaining stakeholder input after receiving an overwhelming number of refugees, but most had not, which made it difficult for health care providers and school systems to prepare for and properly serve refugees.

State and local stakeholders reported that refugees bring cultural diversity and stimulate economic development, but serving refugees can stretch local resources, including safety net services. In addition, refugee students can negatively affect performance outcomes for school districts because they often have limited English proficiency. Furthermore, some refugees choose to relocate after their initial placement, and this secondary migration may stretch communities that do not have adequate resources to serve them. In fact, capacity challenges have led some communities to request restrictions or temporary moratoriums on resettlement.

PRM and the Department of Health and Human Services' Office of Refugee Resettlement (ORR) monitor their refugee assistance programs, but weaknesses in performance measurement may hinder effectiveness. Although refugees are eligible for ORR services for up to 5 years, the outcome data that ORR collects focuses on shorter-term employment outcomes. ORR officials said that their performance measurement reflects the goals outlined by the Immigration and Nationality Act—to help refugees achieve economic self-sufficiency as quickly as possible. However, the focus on rapid employment makes it difficult to provide services that may increase refugees' incomes, such as helping them obtain credentials to practice their professions in the United States.

Little is known about the extent of refugee integration into U.S. communities, but research offers a framework for measuring and facilitating integration. PRM and ORR both promote refugee integration, but neither agency currently measures integration as a program outcome. While integration is part of ORR's mission, ORR officials said one of the reasons they have not measured it is that there is no clear definition of integration. In addition, research on refugee resettlement does not offer an overall assessment of how well refugees have integrated into the United States. Most of the 13 studies GAO reviewed were limited in scope and focused on particular refugee groups in specific geographic locations. However, these studies identified a variety of indicators that can be used to assess integration as well as factors that can facilitate integration, such as English language acquisition, employment, and social support from other refugees. Despite limited national information, some U.S. communities have developed formal plans for refugee integration.

_____ United States Government Accountability Office

Contents

Tables

Figures

Abbreviations

DHS	Department of Homeland Security
HHS	Department of Health and Human Services
ORR	Office of Refugee Resettlement
PRM	Bureau of Population, Refugees, and Migration
State	Department of State

G A O
Accountability * Integrity * Reliability

United States Government Accountability Office
Washington, DC 20548

July 25, 2012

Congressional Requesters

Millions of people worldwide have fled their countries because they have been persecuted—or fear being persecuted—on the basis of their race, religion, nationality, political opinions, or because they belong to a particular social group. The United States has traditionally provided refuge to such people, and continues to resettle at least half of all refugees referred for resettlement worldwide by the United Nations High Commissioner for Refugees each year. In fiscal year 2011, the United States resettled a little more than 56,000 refugees into communities throughout the country. [1]

Nine national voluntary agencies—the nongovernmental organizations that carry out much of the refugee resettlement process with funding from the Departments of State (State) and Health and Human Services (HHS)—take the lead in determining where refugees will initially be placed, with approval from State. The communities in which refugees are placed vary significantly in size, capacity, and experience in resettling refugees. Major gateway cities tend to have more experience incorporating large and steady streams of people from other countries, but can be very expensive places to live. Smaller cities and towns, on the other hand, can be more affordable and easier to navigate, but may not have sufficient resources to provide refugees adequate services, including education and health care. While some refugees stay in the community where they were initially resettled, others may decide to move to another community that may or may not have organizations and programs to help them become self-sufficient.

The most recent economic downturn has made it increasingly difficult for refugees to become self-sufficient within months of arriving in the United States, raising questions about refugee placement and integration, as well as the oversight of refugee resettlement programs. In this context, we were asked to examine (1) the factors resettlement agencies consider when determining where refugees are initially placed; (2) the effects

---

[1] According to data provided by the Department of State, 47 states and the District of Columbia resettled refugees in fiscal year 2011.

refugees have on their communities; (3) how federal agencies ensure the effectiveness and integrity of refugee resettlement programs; and (4) what is known about refugees' integration into the United States.

To address our research objectives, we reviewed relevant federal and state laws, regulations, monitoring protocols, performance reports, performance measures, and other relevant documents. We also conducted a literature review of academic research on the integration of refugees into the United States[2] and reviewed other pertinent reports. We met with federal agency officials, national voluntary agency staff, and experts on refugee programs. In addition, we conducted site visits to eight communities, where we met with representatives from state and local government entities, voluntary agency affiliates, community-based organizations, local businesses, and other relevant individuals and groups, including refugees.[3] For our site visits, we selected Boise, Idaho; Chicago, Illinois; Detroit, Michigan; Fargo, North Dakota; Knoxville, Tennessee; Lancaster, Pennsylvania; Owensboro, Kentucky; and Seattle, Washington.[4] These eight communities represent a nongeneralizable sample that was selected to include geographically distributed communities with variations in their population sizes, levels of experience resettling refugees, and racial and ethnic diversity. In addition to these factors, several communities were selected because they are considered examples of best practices in refugee resettlement by federal officials. For additional information on our scope and methodology, see appendix I.

We conducted this performance audit from May 2011 through July 2012 in accordance with generally accepted government auditing standards. Those standards require that we plan and perform the audit to obtain sufficient, appropriate evidence to provide a reasonable basis for our findings and conclusions based on our audit objectives. We believe that the evidence obtained provides a reasonable basis for our findings and conclusions based on our audit objectives.

---

[2] See appendix II for a list of the studies we included in our literature review.

[3] We did not meet with all of these groups in every community we visited.

[4] As part of our site visit to Chicago, we also met with city officials in Skokie, Illinois. Our visit to the Detroit area focused on the cities of Dearborn and Sterling Heights, Michigan. Our visit to Seattle included interviews with relevant groups in Kent, Washington.

Background

A refugee is generally defined as a person who is outside his or her country and who is unable or unwilling to return because of persecution or a well-founded fear of persecution on account of race, religion, nationality, membership in a particular social group, or political opinion.[5] The Refugee Act of 1980, which amended the Immigration and Nationality Act, provided a systematic and permanent procedure for admitting refugees to the United States and maintains comprehensive and uniform provisions to resettle refugees as quickly as possible and to encourage them to become self-sufficient.[6] Several federal, state, and local government agencies coordinate with private organizations to implement the admission and resettlement process.

Refugee Placement in the United States

Each year the President, after appropriate consultation with the Congress and certain Cabinet members, determines the maximum number of refugees the United States may admit for resettlement in a given year.[7] The number actually resettled is typically below this maximum number

---

[5] 8 U.S.C. § 1101(a)(42)(A). In special circumstances, a refugee also may be a person who is within his or her country and who is persecuted or has a well-founded fear of persecution on account of race, religion, nationality, membership in a particular social group, or political opinion. Excluded from the definition of a refugee is any person who participated in the persecution of another.

[6] The Immigration and Nationality Act is Pub. L. No. 82-414, 66 Stat. 163 (1952) (codified as amended at 8 U.S.C. § 1101 et seq.). The Refugee Act of 1980 is Pub. L. No. 96-212, 94 Stat. 102. While the Immigration and Nationality Act, as amended, states that resettlement programs should help refugees achieve economic self-sufficiency as quickly as possible, it does not define economic self-sufficiency. HHS's Office of Refugee Resettlement defines economic self-sufficiency in its regulations as earning a total family income at a level that enables a family unit to support itself without receipt of a cash assistance grant. 45 C.F.R. § 400.2. Refugees may still be found economically self-sufficient if they receive other types of public noncash assistance, such as Supplemental Nutrition Assistance Program benefits or Medicaid.

[7] The Departments of State, Homeland Security, and Health and Human Services submit a report on behalf of the President to the Congress with their recommendation on how many refugees should be admitted, which according to Department of State officials, takes into account federal agencies' refugee processing capabilities.

and has varied over time—sometimes due to security concerns (see fig. 1).[8]

Figure 1: Presidential Ceilings and Refugee Arrivals (FY 2001-2011)

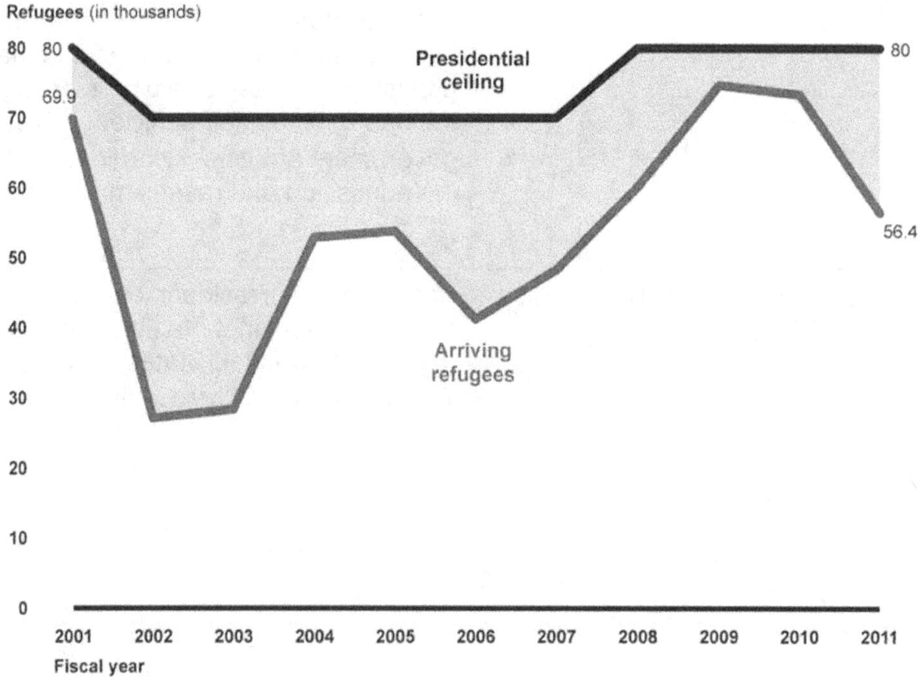

Refugees (in thousands)

Source: GAO analysis of data from Department of State Refugee Processing Center.

The federal government gives private, voluntary agencies responsibility to determine where refugees will live in the United States, with approval

---

[8] The number of refugees entering the United States has increased in recent years compared to the relatively low numbers entering after the terrorist attacks of September 11, 2001. In the aftermath of those attacks, a review of refugee-related security procedures was undertaken, refugee admissions were briefly suspended, and enhanced security measures were implemented. As a result of these and other factors, actual refugee admissions declined from 68,393 in fiscal year 2001 to 26,383 in fiscal year 2002 and 28,348 in fiscal year 2003. Admissions gradually increased and peaked at 74,652 in fiscal year 2009 and leveled off in 2010 with 73,311. Admissions decreased to a little over 56,000 in fiscal year 2011. According to the fiscal year 2012 refugee admissions proposal submitted to Congress by the Departments of State, Homeland Security, and Health and Human Services, this 2011 decrease was due largely to increased security clearance procedures.

from the Department of State. Refugees are assigned first to a national voluntary agency and then the voluntary agency decides where the refugee will live.[9] More specifically, the nine national voluntary agencies, which maintain a network of about 350 affiliates in communities throughout much of the United States, meet weekly to allocate individual refugees based on an annual evaluation of the communities' capacity to serve refugees.[10] See figure 2 for the number of refugees that arrived in each state during fiscal year 2011. Appendix III provides additional detail about the countries of origin for arrivals to the 20 states with the largest refugee populations.

---

[9] According to the Department of State, during weekly allocation meetings, cases with a tie in the United States are allocated to agencies with affiliates in communities where their friends or relatives live. National voluntary agencies then choose cases based on their total proposed capacity as well as local affiliates' capacity and resources. After the allocation meeting, the national voluntary agencies will assign individual cases to local affiliates based on a variety of factors, including ethnicity, language, family size, family composition, or medical conditions. For example, communities with an existing population of a particular ethnicity may have existing infrastructure for serving refugees of a particular ethnicity. Some communities are better able to accommodate larger families, while others may be more hospitable to single households.

[10] According to voluntary agency staff, they identify new communities to receive refugees based on requests from local stakeholders, recommendations by state officials, and the need to expand services to secondary migrants, refugees who migrate from their initial resettlement community to a community in another state.

Figure 2: Refugee Arrivals by State (FY 2011)

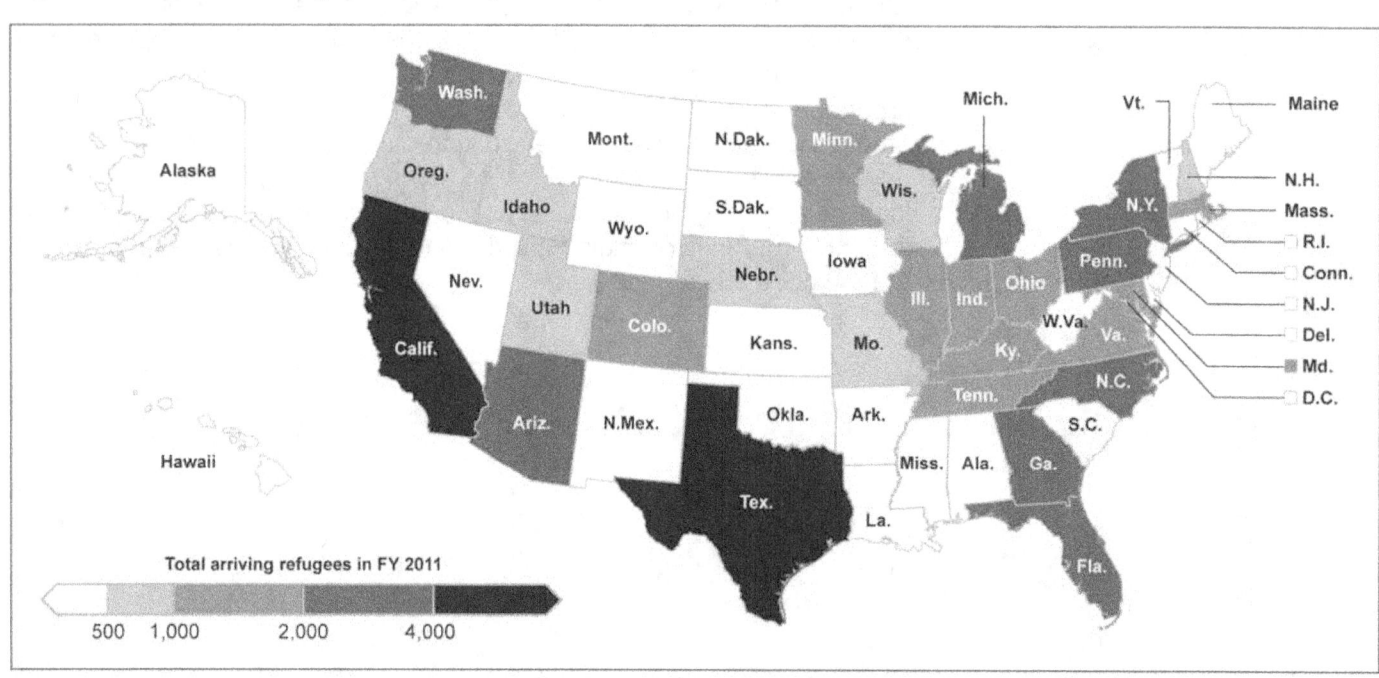

Source: GAO analysis of data from Department of State Refugee Processing Center; National Atlas (base map).

In the last 10 years, refugees have come to the United States from an increasing number of countries, and the issues associated with these diverse populations have become more complex. For example, many refugees today arrive after having lived in refugee camps for years, and may have little formal education or work experience, or untreated medical or mental health conditions. In turn, receiving communities have needed to adjust their language capabilities and services in order to respond to the changing needs of these diverse refugee populations. Figure 3 shows the top 20 countries of origin for refugees arriving in the United States in fiscal year 2011.

Figure 3: Top 20 Countries of Origin for Refugees Arriving FY 2011

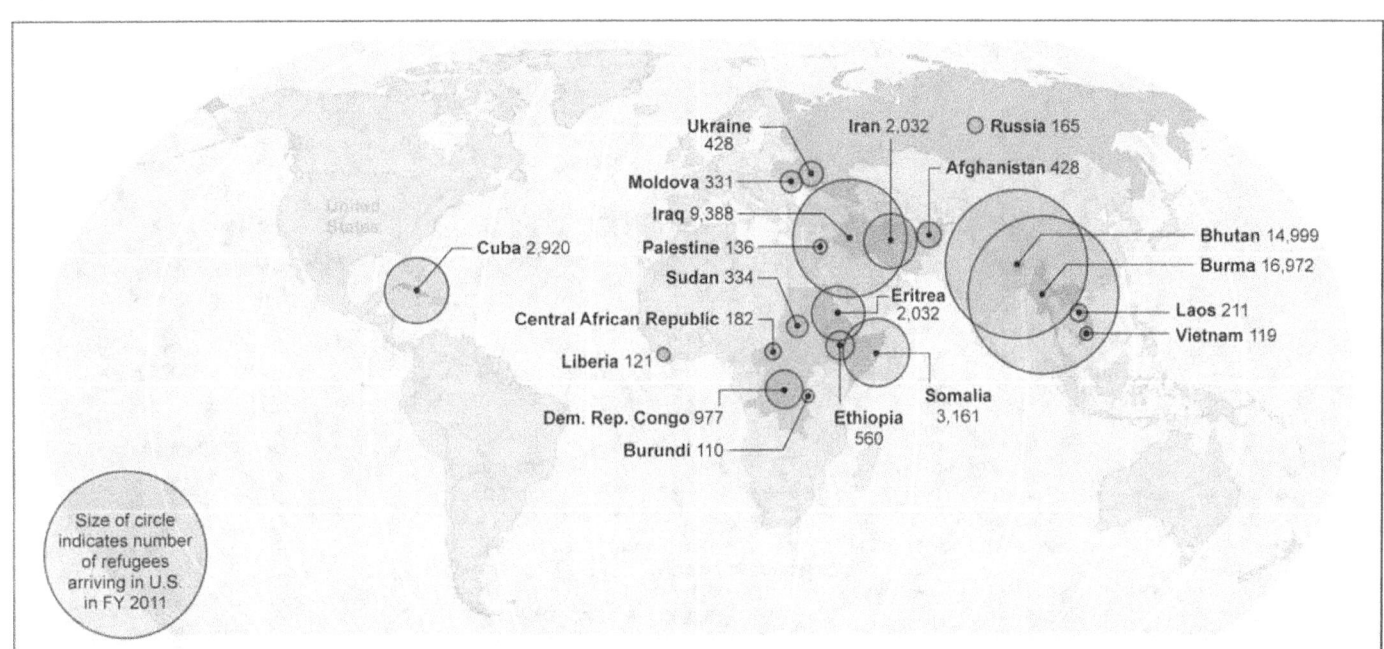

Source: GAO analysis of data from Department of State Refugee Processing Center; National Atlas (base map).

Federal Structure for Refugee Resettlement Programs

Three federal agencies are involved in the refugee resettlement process. The Department of Homeland Security (DHS) approves refugees for admission to the United States. State's Bureau of Population, Refugees, and Migration (PRM) is responsible for processing refugees overseas. Once refugees are processed and arrive in the United States, PRM partially funds services to meet their immediate needs. PRM enters into cooperative agreements with national voluntary agencies under its Reception and Placement Program to provide funding that helps refugees settle into their respective communities during their initial 30 to 90 days and covers housing, food, clothing, and other necessities. Each local affiliate receives $1,850 per refugee to provide these services.[11] Figure 4 illustrates the general path of refugee resettlement in the United States.

[11] Participating organizations are expected to combine PRM's financial assistance with existing and projected private resources for the provision of reception and placement services.

Figure 4: General Path of Refugee Resettlement in the United States

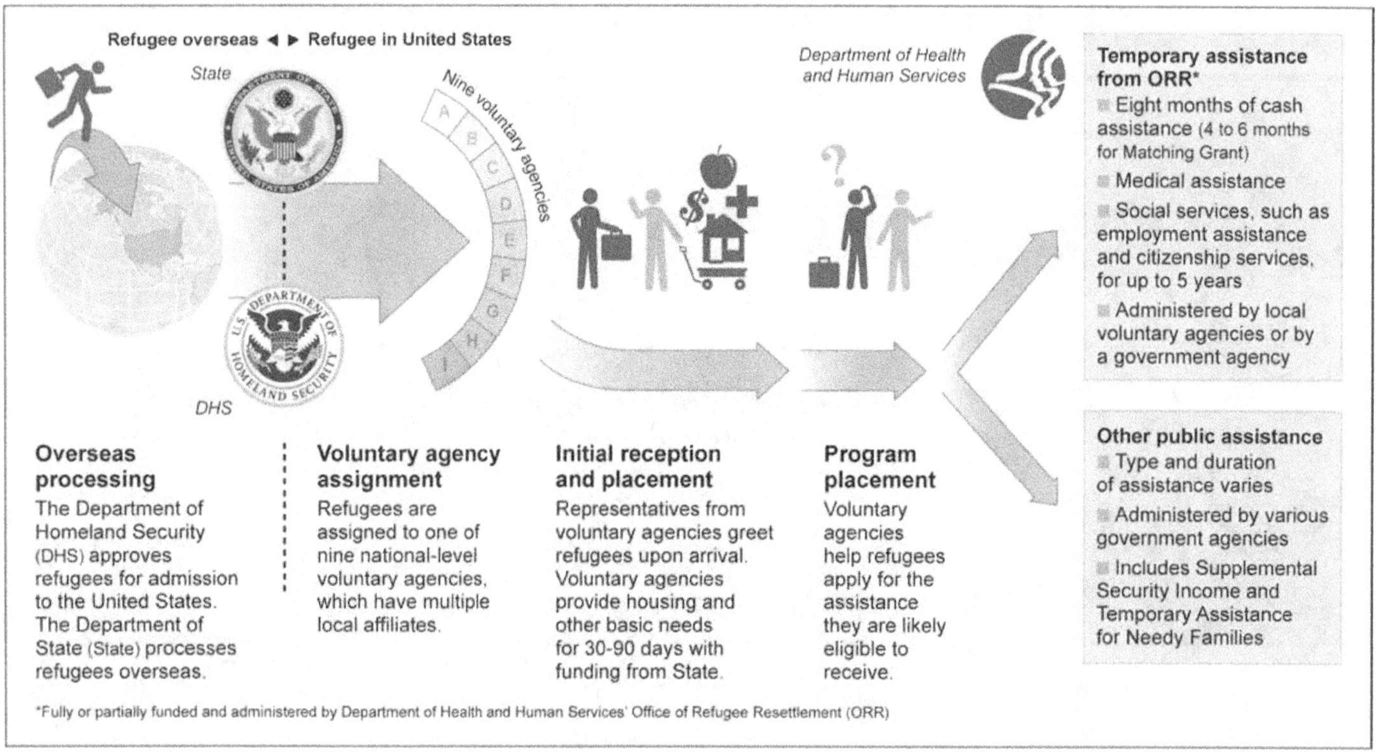

Refugee overseas ◄ ► Refugee in United States

State

Nine voluntary agencies

A B C D E F G H I

DHS

Department of Health and Human Services

Temporary assistance from ORR*
- Eight months of cash assistance (4 to 6 months for Matching Grant)
- Medical assistance
- Social services, such as employment assistance and citizenship services, for up to 5 years
- Administered by local voluntary agencies or by a government agency

Other public assistance
- Type and duration of assistance varies
- Administered by various government agencies
- Includes Supplemental Security Income and Temporary Assistance for Needy Families

Overseas processing

The Department of Homeland Security (DHS) approves refugees for admission to the United States. The Department of State (State) processes refugees overseas.

Voluntary agency assignment

Refugees are assigned to one of nine national-level voluntary agencies, which have multiple local affiliates.

Initial reception and placement

Representatives from voluntary agencies greet refugees upon arrival. Voluntary agencies provide housing and other basic needs for 30-90 days with funding from State.

Program placement

Voluntary agencies help refugees apply for the assistance they are likely eligible to receive.

*Fully or partially funded and administered by Department of Health and Human Services' Office of Refugee Resettlement (ORR)

Source: GAO; National Atlas (globe).

Many refugees are then eligible to receive temporary resettlement assistance from the Office of Refugee Resettlement (ORR), located within HHS. In most states, ORR funds cash and medical assistance as well as social services to help refugees become economically self-sufficient. [12] ORR provides these funds through grants to state refugee coordinators, who may be employed by a state agency or by a nonprofit organization

---

[12] Not all refugees receive cash and medical assistance through ORR-funded programs. Refugees who are eligible for or who are receiving cash assistance from programs outside of ORR, such as Temporary Assistance for Needy Families or Supplemental Security Income, are generally not eligible to receive cash assistance from ORR's resettlement programs.

GAO-12-729 Refugee Resettlement

depending on how a state's program is set up.[13] ORR's social services grants provide funding for employment and other support services. States also receive funding from ORR to award discretionary grants—including school impact, services to older refugees, and targeted assistance grants—to communities that are particularly affected by large numbers of refugees or to serve specific refugee populations such as the elderly. See table 1 for a list of selected refugee assistance programs.

Table 1: Selected Refugee Assistance Programs[a]

Activities	Purpose	FY 2012 budget authority[a] (in millions)
Reception and placement grants	Provides partial financial support to nongovernmental organizations to provide services to refugees for 30 to 90 days after arrival in the United States, including basic needs, orientation, and case management services	$153.7
Transitional and medical services	Provides cash and medical assistance to refugees, asylees, entrants, trafficking victims, and special immigrant visa holders who participate in certain ORR-funded programs.	323.2
Social services	Supports employment and other services such as social adjustment, translation, child care, and citizenship services as well as case management	118.9
Targeted assistance	Primarily provides services designed to secure employment for refugees within 1 year or less in counties that are impacted by high arrival numbers and high concentrations of refugees	24.2
Preventive health	Promotes refugee access to health screening, assessment, treatment, and follow-up services	4.7

Sources: PRM and HHS Administration for Children and Families Justification of Estimates for Appropriations Committees, fiscal year 2013.

---

[13] GAO, *Refugee Assistance: Little is Known about Effectiveness of Different Approaches for Improving Refugees' Employment Outcomes,* GAO-11-369 (Washington, D.C.: Mar. 31, 2011). ORR also partially funds a separate Matching Grant program, administered by the national voluntary agencies. The Matching Grant program provides refugees with cash and other assistance for 4 to 6 months with the goal of helping them become self-sufficient without receiving cash benefits from a public assistance program. According to ORR, refugees who receive assistance from the Matching Grant program may not receive assistance or funding from any of ORR's other three assistance programs at the same time.

ORR also funds targeted grants for unaccompanied alien children, victims of torture, and victims of trafficking. According to ORR, fiscal year 2012 funding levels reflect the reallocation of funding during FY 2012 to support the costs associated with the unprecedented level of Unaccompanied Alien Children referred to HHS/ORR by the Department of Homeland Security during FY 2012.

In addition, communities may apply for grants from other nonrefugee programs to help provide services to refugees. Both PRM and ORR monitor the implementation of the refugee resettlement process, which involves overseeing and monitoring both government agencies and private organizations (see fig. 5).

Figure 5: Flow of Funds from PRM and ORR to Service Providers

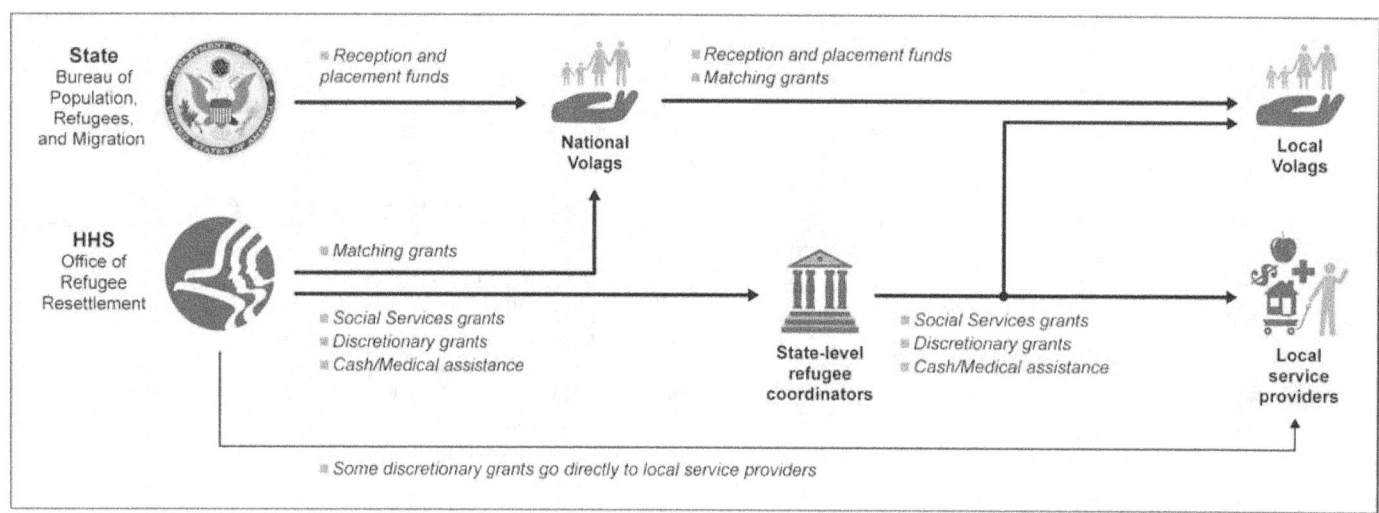

Source: GAO.

ORR and PRM officials coordinate with one another and with national and state stakeholders who specifically focus on serving refugees. Together with representatives from national resettlement agencies and state refugee coordinators, ORR and PRM also participate in a refugee resettlement working group convened by the White House National Security Staff, which supports both the Homeland Security Council and the National Security Council. The resettlement working group has worked on and been supportive of a variety of reforms that PRM and ORR have made to their processes. PRM and ORR also conduct joint quarterly consultation meetings with stakeholder groups, including voluntary agencies, state refugee coordinators, refugee health coordinators, ORR technical assistance providers, and ethnic community based organizations.

Voluntary Agencies Consider Various Factors in Placing Refugees, but Few Consult with Local Service Providers

Voluntary Agencies Consider Various Factors When Making Refugee Placement Decisions

Voluntary agencies consider a variety of factors when they propose the number of refugees to be resettled in each community (see table 2). Before preparing their annual proposals for PRM's Reception and Placement Program for approval, national voluntary agencies ask local voluntary agency affiliates to assess their own capacity and that of other service providers in the wider community and propose the number of refugees that they will be able to resettle that year.[14] In making these assessments, local voluntary agency affiliates typically consider both their own internal capacity and the capacity of the community, with different levels of emphasis on one or the other.[15] For example, when determining how many refugees their community can accommodate, local affiliates in one community told us that they primarily consider their internal capacity—such as staffing levels, staff skills, long-term funding needs, the number of refugees they have served in the past, and success in meeting refugee employment goals in the previous year. Local affiliates in another community explained that they primarily consider community-based factors, such as housing availability and employment opportunities. To help make this process more consistent, Refugee Council USA, a coalition of the nine national voluntary agencies, developed guidance and a list of factors that local affiliates could use when evaluating community capacity. However, national voluntary agencies do not require their local

---

[14] The proposals typically include information on community capacity—such as employment rates, available healthcare, and housing—as well as information on the voluntary agency's organizational management plans and policies. PRM reviews and approves proposals from the national voluntary agencies.

[15] While some local affiliates may gather information about community-based factors by consulting with local stakeholders, others may choose to review publicly available information, such as the unemployment rate and rental prices.

affiliates to use the guidance. Moreover, national voluntary agencies may adjust the numbers proposed by local affiliates.

Because refugees are generally placed in communities where national voluntary agency affiliates have been successful in resettling refugees, the same communities are often asked to absorb refugees year after year. One state refugee coordinator noted that local affiliate funding is based on the number of refugees they serve, so affiliates have an incentive to maintain or increase the number of refugees they resettle each year rather than allowing the number to decrease.

Table 2: Sample Factors That Voluntary Agencies Consider When Assessing Community Capacity

Community factors	Internal factors
Employment opportunities	Language ability of staff
Availability of affordable housing	Staff size (ratio of staff to refugees)
Existing ethnic and linguistic groups	Number of Matching Grant program slots
Public transportation	Volunteer corps
Health care resources	Private revenue
State budget trends for public assistance	Long-term financial needs of the organization
Number of available co-sponsors	

Source: GAO analysis of PRM, Refugee Council USA guidance, and interviews with voluntary agency officials.

Given Limited Guidance, Few Voluntary Agencies We Visited Sought Input from Relevant Community Stakeholders When Placing Refugees

Even though they are required to coordinate and consult with state and local governments about their resettlement activities, voluntary agencies have received only limited guidance from PRM on how to obtain input from these and other community stakeholders when assessing communities' capacity. The Immigration and Nationality Act, as amended, states that it is the intent of Congress that local voluntary agency activities should be conducted in close cooperation and advance consultation with state and local governments,[16] and the cooperative agreements that the Department of State enters into with national voluntary agencies require the agencies to conduct their reception and placement activities in this

---

[16] 8 U.S.C. § 1522(a)(1)(B)(iii).

manner.[17] Driven by concerns that voluntary agencies were not consulting sufficiently with state and local stakeholders when developing their proposals, PRM directed local voluntary agencies to do more to document consultations with state and local stakeholders regarding the communities' capacity to serve refugees.[18] However, PRM's guidance on consultation with state and local governments does not provide detailed information regarding the agency's expectations for the content of these discussions. While the guidance provides some examples of state and local stakeholders that the voluntary agencies could potentially consult, it does not state which stakeholders must be consulted. PRM officials said that they allow local voluntary agencies to decide whom to consult because the voluntary agencies know their communities best and because local circumstances vary.

Most local voluntary agencies we visited have not taken steps to ensure that other relevant service providers are afforded the opportunity to provide input on the number and types of refugees that can be served. As a result, many local service providers experienced challenges in properly serving refugees. Most of the local voluntary agencies told us they generally consult with private stakeholders such as apartment landlords or potential employers prior to resettling refugees in an area. They also stated that they consult with some public entities, such as state refugee coordinators; however, most public entities such as public schools and health departments generally said that voluntary agencies notified them of the number of refugees expected to arrive in the coming year, but did not consult them regarding the number of refugees they could serve before proposals were submitted to PRM. Moreover, service providers in one community noted that because the local voluntary agencies did not

---

[17] The cooperative agreements provide the conditions that the recipient must meet in exchange for receiving federal funding. The agreements signed by the national voluntary agencies also require them to ensure that their local affiliates participate in meetings called by state and local governments to coordinate plans for the placement of refugees. Similarly, ORR's regulations require states to provide an assurance in their state plan for refugee resettlement funds that local voluntary agencies and other community service agencies will meet with state and local governments at least quarterly to coordinate the appropriate placement of refugees in advance of the refugees' arrival. 45 C.F.R. § 400.5(h).

[18] For example, in fiscal year 2009, PRM required the voluntary agencies to provide the date and content of discussions with state and local stakeholders. In fiscal year 2010, PRM added a requirement for the voluntary agencies to include the results of those discussions. In 2012, PRM required voluntary agencies to include any concerns raised and compromises reached.

consult them on the numbers and ethnicities of refugees they were planning to resettle, there were no interpreters or residents that spoke the language of some of the refugees who were resettled there, even though the providers could have served refugees that spoke other languages.

Voluntary agencies may not consult with relevant stakeholders if they perceive them to be unaware of the resettlement process or if they believe that refugees do not use certain services. For example, local voluntary agency staff in one community said they did not consult with certain stakeholders because they believed that they were not well informed about the resettlement process and might unnecessarily object to the proposed number of refugees to be resettled. In fact, one local, elected official we spoke to was unaware that refugees were living in the community. Other elected officials noted that it was difficult to tell if or when refugees accessed services, even though school and health department officials in those same communities had frequent interactions with refugees and wanted opportunities to provide input.

Although they bear much of the responsibility for providing services to refugees, some of the health care providers and schools that had not been consulted on, or even notified of, the number of refugees that were to be resettled sometimes felt unprepared to do so. For example, health care providers in two communities told us that they were not notified in advance that refugees would be arriving in their communities, and thus, had no time to set up screening procedures. They were also unaware of the specific needs and health challenges of the communities they were serving.

In addition, in some instances when voluntary agencies were unable to adequately prepare the community as a whole for the new arrivals and provide refugees with the services they needed, some community members expressed opposition toward the refugees. For example, in Fort Wayne, Indiana, a few case studies show that the community, which had been receiving fewer than 500 refugees per year prior to 2007, experienced a rapid increase that more than tripled the number of refugees resettled in the community.[19] The community, in turn, was forced on short notice to obtain new sources of funding and establish a new infrastructure in order to serve their new arrivals. This unplanned increase in refugees, combined with a growing unemployment rate, engendered frustrations that resulted in backlash from the community. Moreover, a number of other factors, including the high frequency of communicable diseases among certain populations, unmet needs for mental health services, overcrowding in homes, and cultural practices caused existing residents to become concerned or even hostile. Similarly, officials in Clarkston, Georgia, another community that was not initially consulted regarding the resettlement of thousands of refugees beginning in 1996, described the flight of long-time residents from the town in response to refugee resettlement and the perceived deterioration of the quality of schools.[20]

In a few of the communities we visited, after reaching a crisis point due to the influx of refugees, stakeholders took the initiative to develop formal processes for providing input to the local voluntary agencies on the number of refugees they could serve.[21] For example, an influx of refugees in Fargo, North Dakota, in the 1990s overwhelmed local service providers. In response, those service providers and the local voluntary agency formed a Refugee Advisory Committee to provide a formal, community-based structure for finding solutions to challenges in resettling refugees. The committee includes representatives from the local voluntary agency, state and county social services departments, various city departments, school districts, as well as local health care providers,

---

[19] General Dynamics Information Technology, Inc., *Building an Integrated Refugee Program*, a report prepared at the request of the Department of Health and Human Services Office of Refugee Resettlement (ORR), November 2009. Staff of Senate Committee on Foreign Relations, 111th Cong., Abandoned Upon Arrival: Implications for Refugees and Local Communities Burdened by a U.S. Resettlement System That is Not Working (Comm. Print 2010).

[20] According to PRM, in the past five years, affiliate abstracts submitted in annual proposals detail consultations and ongoing work with various state and local entities concerning placement in Clarkston. These consultations include regular meetings of the Georgia Coalition of Refugee Stakeholders, whose members include local elected officials. They also note discussions regarding housing, health services, and public school issues and consultations with the DeKalb county Board of Health/Refugee Clinic director and the DeKalb County school system. By request of the State Refugee Coordinator, in fiscal year 2011, refugee placements in Clarkston were reduced.

[21] These communities were recommended to us as examples of best practices.

nonprofit organizations, and the assistant state refugee coordinator. The local voluntary agency solicits input from the committee annually on the number of refugees the community has the capacity to serve in the coming year and also meets quarterly to address other issues such as the needs of service providers. Committee members told us that the number of new refugees arriving in Fargo declined after the committee was developed.[22] Committee members and voluntary agency officials said that their close communication allows them to better educate the community and better serve the refugees, and both believe the number being resettled is manageable.

Similarly, in Boise, Idaho, city officials formed a roundtable group to develop a Refugee Resource Strategic Community Plan in 2009 to work with the local voluntary agencies, the state refugee coordinator's office, and community organizations to identify strategies for successful resettlement of Boise's refugees, in light of the most recent economic downturn. The group includes representatives from the state coordinator's office, local voluntary agencies, various city departments, school district representatives, nonprofit organizations, as well as employers, health care providers, and other community stakeholders. The group meets quarterly to review progress on the objectives outlined in the strategic plan. The local voluntary agencies obtain input from the group members on the community's capacity for serving refugees, but they do not discuss the specific number of refugees that will be proposed to the national voluntary agency and PRM for resettlement. Roundtable members told us that the local voluntary agencies have worked with their national offices to reduce the proposed number of refugees to resettle in Boise in 2011 based on community capacity.

The state of Tennessee has passed legislation that creates formal processes for communication between voluntary agencies and local stakeholders. Specifically, the Refugee Absorptive Capacity Act,[23] which was passed in 2011, requires the state refugee program office to enter into a letter of agreement with each voluntary agency in the state. The

---

[22] Data from the voluntary agency show that the number of newly arriving refugees in Fargo and West Fargo declined from 564 in fiscal year 2000 to 327 in fiscal year 2001 and to 42 in fiscal year 2002. Over the next 8 years, the number of new arrivals increased, but remained below the fiscal year 2000 level. In fiscal year 2010, there were 356 new arrivals.

[23] Codified at Tenn. Code Ann. §§ 4-38-101 to 4-38-104.

letter of agreement must contain a requirement that local stakeholders mutually consult and prepare a plan for the initial placement of refugees in a community as well as a plan for ongoing consultation. In addition, the state program office must ensure that local voluntary agencies consult upon request with local governments regarding refugee placement in advance of the refugees' arrival.[24]

Refugees Bring Benefits to Communities but Can Pose Challenges for Service Providers

Refugees Bring Diversity and Can Help Stimulate Development, but Can Stretch Resources and Affect Program Outcomes

Communities can benefit socially and economically from refugee resettlement. In all of the communities we visited, stakeholders said that refugees enriched their cultural diversity. For example, local service providers in Fargo commented that refugees bring new perspectives and customs to a city with predominately Norwegian ancestry. Some city officials and business leaders we spoke with in several communities said that refugees help stimulate economic development by filling critical labor shortages as well as by starting small businesses and creating jobs. For instance, new refugee-owned businesses revitalized a neighborhood in Chicago after other businesses in the area closed. In addition, an official in Washington State told us that diverse resettlement communities with international populations attract investment from overseas businesses. According to ORR officials, refugees also bring economic benefits to communities by renting apartments, patronizing local businesses, and paying taxes, and the presence of refugees may increase the amount of federal funding that a community receives.[25] In Boise, officials

---

[24] The law also requires the state program office to provide a written quarterly report to local governments to plan and coordinate the placement of refugees, provide a quarterly report to specified state legislative committees, and ensure that host community residents and representatives of local governments are aware that they should notify the state program office with any concerns about resettlement activities.

[25] ORR officials noted, for example, that schools might receive additional federal funding if the proportion of low-income students in a school increases.

commented that the refugee students helped stabilize the public school population, which had been declining before the city established a refugee resettlement program.

While refugees can benefit their communities, they can also stretch the resources of local service providers, such as school districts and health care systems. In several communities we visited, school district officials said that it takes more resources to serve refugee students than nonrefugee students, because they sometimes lack formal schooling or have experienced trauma, which can require additional supports, such as special training for school staff. In addition, newly arrived refugee students often have limited English proficiency, and hiring interpreters can be costly.[26] Similarly, some health care providers expressed concerns about serving refugees, because they said that they are required to provide interpreter services to patients with limited English proficiency.[27] One provider told us that their clinic spent more than $100,000 on interpreter services in the previous year, costs that were not reimbursed.[28] In addition, in some communities we visited, school district officials and health care providers said that locating interpreters for certain languages can be difficult. ORR and PRM officials noted that these impacts are not unique to refugees and that serving immigrants may pose similar challenges.

ORR offers discretionary grants to assist school districts that serve a large number of refugees, but we learned that district officials may be

---

[26] According to ORR officials, the Department of Education provides supplemental funding under Title III of the Elementary and Secondary Education Act, as amended, Language Instruction for Limited English Proficient and Immigrant Students. However, school district officials in one community we visited said that continuous cuts in Title III funding have had significant impacts on schools that serve refugee students.

[27] ORR's regulations require that in providing refugee medical assistance, states must provide at least the same services in the same manner and to the same extent as under the state's Medicaid program. In addition, all recipients of federal funds are required to comply with Title VI of the Civil Rights Act of 1964, which prohibits discrimination based on race, color, or national origin under any program receiving federal financial assistance. Several health care providers and voluntary agencies we spoke with viewed the hiring of interpreters as a way to comply with this requirement. This report, however, does not attempt to assess entities' compliance with Title VI requirements.

[28] Under Medicaid, states may claim federal matching funds for interpreter costs; however, in this case, the amount reimbursed by the state Medicaid program covered approximately half of the cost of the interpreter services, which left the provider to cover the remaining cost.

unaware of these grants or may decide that the effort involved in applying for them outweighs the potential benefits. For example, through its school impact grant, ORR funds activities for refugee students such as English as a Second Language instruction and after-school tutorials. However, school district officials in one community that was new to the refugee resettlement program said they had no information about where they could find assistance in serving refugee students. In another community, district officials were aware of the school impact grant, but said they did not apply for it because they found the application process to be burdensome and the funding level would have been insufficient to meet their needs.[29]

In addition to stretching school district resources, refugee students can also negatively affect district performance outcomes. School district performance is measured primarily by students' test scores, including the scores of refugee students. School district officials in several communities said that even though refugee students often have limited English proficiency, they are evaluated against the same metrics as their native English-speaking peers, which can result in lower performance outcomes for the district. In one community, officials told us that the district had not demonstrated adequate yearly progress under the state standards in recent years, and they attributed this in part to the test scores of refugee students. [30]

Furthermore, refugees who exhaust federal refugee assistance benefits and are not self-sufficient can strain local safety nets. Refugees who are no longer eligible to receive cash and medical assistance from ORR after 8 months but are unemployed—or are working in low-wage jobs that do not provide sufficient income—may seek help from local service providers such as food pantries, organizations providing housing assistance, and even homeless shelters. If service providers are unprepared to serve these refugees in addition to their other clients, it can stretch their

---

[29] For fiscal year 2012, the school impact grant program provided funding to states ranging from $150,000 to $1 million, depending on the size of the school-age refugee population and other eligible populations. States used these funds to award grants to state departments of education, local school districts, or voluntary agencies.

[30] Under the Elementary and Secondary Education Act, as amended, all students are expected to meet or exceed state standards in reading and in math by 2014. Each state establishes its own definition of adequate yearly progress to determine school and school district achievement toward this goal.

budgets and diminish the safety net resources available to others in the community.

Table 3 lists the benefits and challenges of refugee resettlement identified by stakeholders in the communities we visited.

Table 3: Benefits and Challenges of Refugee Resettlement Identified in Site Visits

Benefits	Challenges
Refugees add diversity to their communities	Communication can be difficult due to language and cultural barriers
The presence of refugees in a community teaches tolerance for others	Mental health resources are limited for refugees who have experienced trauma
Refugees take jobs that are difficult to fill	The cost of interpreter services can strain service providers' budgets, and some health care providers have chosen to stop serving refugees
Refugees are reliable, dedicated employees	
Refugee-owned businesses create jobs	Refugee students with limited English proficiency can affect school districts' performance outcomes
Public services developed to assist refugees, such as transit programs, also benefit other vulnerable populations	Some refugees live in poverty due to unemployment
	Some refugees are unfamiliar with social norms and laws in the United States

Source: GAO interviews with stakeholders in selected communities.

Some Refugees Relocate after Resettlement, and This Secondary Migration May Strain Communities That Lack Adequate Resources to Serve Them

Migration from one community to another after initial resettlement—referred to as secondary migration—can unexpectedly increase the refugee population in a community, and communities that attract large numbers of secondary migrants may not have adequate, timely funding to provide resettlement services to the migrants who need them.[31] According to ORR, refugees relocate for a variety of reasons: better employment opportunities, the pull of an established ethnic community, more welfare benefits, better training opportunities, reunification with

---

[31] According to PRM officials, refugees often migrate multiple times. Officials also noted that some refugees who choose to migrate from their initial resettlement communities do so within a few months of arrival, while others do so after a longer period of time.

relatives, or a more congenial climate.[32] Not all refugees who migrate choose to access resettlement services in their new communities, according to PRM officials. However, for those migrants who need resettlement services, federal funding does not necessarily follow them to their new communities, even though refugees continue to be eligible for some resettlement services for 5 years after arrival. According to ORR officials, refugees who relocate while they are receiving cash assistance, medical assistance, or refugee social services are eligible to continue receiving those services in their new communities for a limited time.[33] However, ORR does not coordinate this continuation of service, and state refugee coordinators must communicate with one another to determine eligibility for each refugee who relocates.

In addition, ORR provides grants to communities and states affected by secondary migration, but the annual cycle of these grants may not provide ORR the flexibility to respond in a timely manner. ORR uses secondary migration data submitted by states once a year, among other data, to inform refugee social services funding allocations for future fiscal years. [34] According to ORR officials, these formula grants are awarded annually to states based on the number of refugee arrivals during the previous 2 years. As a result, a year may pass before states experiencing

---

[32] According to PRM data for fiscal year 2011, 3,261 refugees, or 5.7 percent of refugees, moved away from their initial resettlement community within the first 90 days of resettlement. According to ORR data for fiscal year 2010, states reported that approximately 11,143 refugees moved from their initial resettlement state. ORR collects secondary migration data on refugees who have arrived within 36 months prior to the beginning of the fiscal year. Fiscal year 2010 data showed that Texas and California had large numbers of refugees moving both in and out. There was strong net migration into Minnesota, Florida, Colorado, Ohio, and Kansas. There was strong net migration out of Arizona, New York, New Jersey, Texas, and Georgia.

[33] Depending on the program in which they are enrolled, refugees are eligible to receive ORR-funded cash assistance for 8 months if they are enrolled in a statewide program. Refugees enrolled in a Matching Grant program are eligible to receive cash assistance for 4 to 6 months after arrival. Refugees are also eligible for ORR-funded medical assistance for up to 8 months after arrival. Refugees are eligible to receive services through ORR's social services grant program for up to 5 years after arrival.

[34] Refugee social services programs provide employment and other services such as social adjustment, translation, childcare, and citizenship services, as well as case management. ORR allocates these funds to states based on estimates of arriving refugees, as well as secondary migration data for the prior 2 years. These social services funds do not increase within a given year if the number of refugees served is greater than anticipated.

secondary migration receive increased funding. For example, Minnesota reported to ORR that 1,999 refugees migrated into the state during fiscal year 2010, but under ORR's current formula funding process, the state would not have received increased funding until fiscal year 2011. In another example, social services funding did not keep pace with a large number of arrivals of both newly resettled refugees and secondary migrants in Detroit in fiscal year 2008. According to a report commissioned by ORR, after this rapid influx of arrivals, caseloads rose to 150 clients per caseworker in the employment and training program, and caseworkers were forced to devote a majority of their time to paperwork and case management, which limited their ability to provide job development and training services.[35] Further, ORR will not adjust a state's level of social services funding to account for secondary migration until it verifies that the refugees migrated to the state. According to one state refugee coordinator, ORR rejects the data states submit if the refugee's information does not match the information in ORR's database or if two or more states claim to have served the same refugee. ORR officials said that, while their process allows states to update missing data and correct formatting errors, it does not allow states to resubmit data that does not match the information in ORR's database or that was submitted by two or more states.[36]

ORR offers supplemental, short-term funding to help communities affected by secondary migration. For example, the Supplemental Services for Recently Arrived Refugees grant is designed to help communities provide services to secondary migrants or newly arriving refugees when the communities are not sufficiently prepared in terms of linguistic or culturally appropriate services or do not have sufficient service capacity. However, this grant is only available to communities that will serve a minimum of 100 refugees annually, and the funding is for a fixed period of time.[37] Communities must apply and be approved for the

---

[35] General Dynamics Information Technology, Inc., *Building an Integrated Refugee Program*.

[36] According to ORR officials, less than 10 percent of the data submitted on secondary migrants are rejected.

[37] To be considered for the Supplemental Services for Recently Arrived Refugees grant, communities must demonstrate situations such as (1) refugee services do not presently exist or the service capacity is not sufficient to accommodate significant increases in arrivals; and/or (2) the existing service system does not have culturally and linguistically appropriate services. ORR provides grantees with funding for a grant project period of 17 months.

grant, and funding may not arrive until many months after the influx began. For example, in a draft report on secondary migration commissioned by ORR, the Spring Institute for Intercultural Learning found that one community did not receive supplemental funding until 14 months after secondary migrant refugees began arriving.[38]

Without comprehensive secondary migration data, ORR cannot target supplemental assistance to communities and refugees in a timely way. Currently, the data that PRM and ORR collect on secondary migration are limited and little is known about secondary migration patterns. PRM collects data from local voluntary agencies regarding the number of refugees who move away from a community within the first 90 days after arrival, but does not collect data on the estimated number of refugees who enter the community during the same time period. PRM officials said that they use these out-migration data to assess the success of refugee placement decisions. In contrast, ORR collects secondary migration data annually from each state, but does not collect community-level data. Specifically, ORR collects information on the number of refugees who move into and out of each state every year. However, ORR officials explained that they can only collect these data when secondary migrants access services. As a result, refugees who move into or out of a state but do not use refugee services in their new communities are not counted. Even so, these refugees access other community services and their communities may need additional assistance to meet their needs.

Secondary migration can strain local resources significantly. For example, the draft report on secondary migration prepared for ORR by the Spring Institute for Intercultural Learning found that refugees who migrate to new communities can overwhelm local service providers, such as health departments, that are unprepared to serve them. In addition, a report prepared for ORR by General Dynamics Information Technology, Inc. found that, in one community, the influx of a large number of secondary migrants who lacked resources led to a homelessness crisis that stressed

---

[38] Spring Institute for Intercultural Learning. *Rural Secondary Migration Pilot Project: Impacts, Challenges, and Opportunities,*, a report prepared at the request of the Department of Health and Human Services Office of Refugee Resettlement (ORR), October 2009.

the capacity of both the shelter system and the other agencies serving refugees.[39]

Capacity Challenges Can Lead Communities to Request Restrictions or Temporary Moratoriums on Refugee Resettlement

Some communities that face challenges in serving additional refugees have requested restrictions or even temporary moratoriums on refugee resettlement. According to PRM, the cities of Detroit and Fort Wayne, Indiana, requested restrictions on refugee resettlement due to poor economic conditions. In response, PRM limited resettlement in Detroit and Fort Wayne to refugees who already have family there.[40] In addition, the mayor of Manchester, New Hampshire, asked in 2011 that PRM temporarily stop resettling refugees in the city because of a shortage of jobs and sufficient affordable housing. While PRM did not grant the requested moratorium, the agency reduced the number of refugees to be resettled there in fiscal year 2011 from 300 to about 200. PRM officials said that a moratorium on resettlement would not have made sense because nearly all of the refugees slated to be resettled in Manchester have family there and would likely relocate to Manchester eventually—even if they were initially settled in another location.

Tennessee recently created a process by which communities could request a temporary moratorium on refugee resettlement for capacity reasons. The state's Refugee Absorptive Capacity Act allows local governments to submit a request to the state refugee office for a 1-year moratorium on resettling additional refugees if they document that they lack the capacity to do so and if further resettlement would have an adverse impact on residents. The state refugee office may then forward this request to PRM.[41] Passed in 2011, the law states that local governments should consider certain capacity factors—the capacity of service providers to meet existing needs of current residents, the

---

[39] General Dynamics Information Technology, Inc., *Building an Integrated Refugee Program.*

[40] PRM initially limited resettlement in these cities to immediate family members of refugees who were already living there. However, in response to requests from the local voluntary agencies and a leveling in the flow of arrivals, the metro Detroit policy was amended to allow placement of any refugees with ties to family or friends in the area. According to voluntary agency officials, the policy was amended due to high levels of secondary migration and the difficulty serving secondary migrants without funding.

[41] PRM has discretion to approve or deny this request, as state law is not binding on the federal government.

availability of affordable housing, the capacity of the school district to meet the needs of refugee students, and the ability of the local economy to absorb new workers—before making such a request. According to PRM, to date, no community in Tennessee has submitted such a request.

Agencies Monitor Resettlement and Measure Effectiveness, but These Measures Have Weaknesses

PRM and ORR Take Different Approaches to Program Oversight

PRM conducts regular on-site monitoring of national voluntary agencies and about 350 local affiliates to ensure that the voluntary agencies deliver the services outlined in their cooperative agreements. Under the cooperative agreements, local voluntary agencies must provide certain services to refugees in the first 30 to 90 days after they arrive. PRM monitors national voluntary agencies annually and local affiliates once every 5 years, and requires national voluntary agencies to monitor their affiliates at least once every 3 years. During its local affiliate monitoring visits, PRM reviews case files and interviews staff. PRM officials also visit a small sample of refugees in their homes to ensure that the refugees received clean, safe housing and appropriate furniture. PRM also requires voluntary agencies to report certain outcome measures for each refugee they resettle.

In recent years, PRM found most local affiliates generally compliant, and for those that were not, PRM made recommendations and required immediate corrective action. For fiscal years 2009 through 2011, according to PRM, it conducted 136 on-site monitoring visits. In over three-quarters of those visits, PRM determined that the local affiliate was compliant or mostly compliant. In about one-quarter of the cases, however, PRM determined that they were partially or mostly noncompliant (about 20 percent) or simply noncompliant (about 5 percent). PRM or national resettlement agencies can make return, on-site monitoring trips to assess the progress of affiliates when problems are identified. Furthermore, if the problems persist, national voluntary agencies can close an affiliate's operation or PRM can decide not to allow placement of refugees at an affiliate. For fiscal year 2011, PRM determined that the most common recommendation made to local affiliates was that the local affiliate should document the reason core services could not be provided in the required time frames. (See table 4 for the top 10 recommendations made for fiscal year 2011.)

Table 4: Top 10 Recommendations for FY 2011 from PRM Monitoring Visits

1.	Ensure that when core services cannot be completed within the time frames specified in the Cooperative Agreement, the case note logs specify the reason for the delay.
2.	Ensure that services are provided with interpretation, as needed, that allows for communication with the refugee in his/her native language or in a common language in which the refugee is fluent, throughout the reception and placement period.
3.	Take immediate steps to ensure that infestation noted in home visits is addressed.
4.	Conduct at least two home visits for each case: the initial home visit within 24 hours, as well as an additional home visit within 30 days of arrival.
5.	Ensure that refugees receive all essential furnishings upon arrival.
6.	Ensure that a resettlement plan is developed for each refugee, including children, that indicates the initial assessment of employability for each employable refugee and includes a clear plan of action based on an assessment of the individual.
7.	The headquarters should have in place a formal plan for training new headquarters staff and affiliate directors, and should ensure that each affiliate has a structured training plan for each of its new employees.
8.	The affiliate should ensure that culturally appropriate, ready-to-eat food is available upon a refugee's arrival, plus one day's worth of additional food supplies. The affiliate should provide food or food allowance at least equivalent to the food stamp allocation continued food assistance until receipt of food stamps or until the individual or family is able to provide his or her own food.
9.	Ensure minor suitability determinations are completed within 1 week of the minor's arrival, and that minors' files are segregated and can be readily identified.
10.	Ensure that every refugee has a health assessment within 30 days of arrival and that refugees with acute health care requirements receive appropriate and timely medical attention.

Source: PRM.

Whereas PRM's oversight focuses on services provided, ORR's oversight focuses more on performance outcomes. In order to assess the performance of its programs that provide cash, medical assistance, and social services to refugees, ORR monitors employment outcomes and cash assistance terminations (see table 5). It uses a similar set of measures for its Matching Grant program.

Table 5: Performance Outcome Measures for Major Refugee Assistance Programs

Statewide Measures[a]	Matching Grant program
1. Entered Employment	1. Entered Employment
2. Average Wage at Employment	2. Average Wage at Employment
3. Employment with Health Benefits	3. Employment with Health Benefits
4. Job Retention for 90 days	4. Self-Sufficient at 120th day
5. Cash Assistance Reductions due to Earnings	5. Economic Self-Sufficiency Retention at the 180th day
6. Cash Assistance Termination due to Earnings	6. Economic Self-Sufficiency Overall

Source: ORR program guidance.

[a]ORR prepares an Annual Performance Plan, which presents goals and progress toward six measures of economic self-sufficiency. Each state negotiates with ORR to establish a target for each measure, and states are encouraged to set or negotiate similar targets with programs within the state. ORR uses these measures for all statewide programs—publicly administered, public private partnerships, and Wilson-Fish programs, which are administered by a voluntary agency. For more information on the statewide programs, see GAO-11-369.

According to ORR, its focus on employment outcomes as a measure of effectiveness is based on the Immigration and Nationality Act, as amended, which requires ORR to help refugees attain economic self-sufficiency as soon as possible.[42] ORR considers refugees self-sufficient if they earn enough income that enables the family to support itself without cash assistance—even if they receive other types of noncash public assistance, such as Supplemental Nutrition Assistance Program benefits or Medicaid.[43]

ORR conducts its on-site monitoring at the state level to ensure the program is able to collect and report accurate data and to ensure that the state is able to provide services to refugees. ORR's on-site monitoring identifies deficiencies as well as best practices. ORR generally monitors state refugee coordinators onsite once every 3 years, as the state coordinator is responsible for administering and overseeing ORR's major grants. During the on-site visit, ORR also monitors a sample of subgrantees. In monitoring reports from its most recent on-site monitoring

[42]8 U.S.C. § 1522(a)(1)(A)(i). This law requires ORR to do so to the extent of available appropriations.

[43]Cash assistance includes both refugee cash assistance and payments received under the Temporary Assistance for Needy Families program.

in the states we visited, ORR identified a number of deficiencies including:

- failure to inform refugees that they were eligible for certain services for up to 5 years,
- failure to ensure that medical assistance was terminated at the end of the 8-month eligibility period,
- failure to ensure that translators were available when providing services to refugees, and
- missing documentation in case files.

The monitoring reports contained ORR's recommendations and noted when corrective action was required. ORR's monitoring reports also identified program strengths and best practices that monitors observed while on site. For example, one ORR monitoring report noted that having a state refugee housing coordinator was a program strength, because this coordinator can locate affordable housing and research funding sources, which saves the caseworkers time and effort. In the same state, ORR found that having an employment specialist at a voluntary agency who can help refugees obtain job upgrades and pursue professional certificates was also a program strength. According to ORR officials, they supplement this on-site monitoring with desk monitoring, which may include reviews of case files, or reviews of information provided in periodic reports.

Neither ORR nor PRM has formal mechanisms for collecting and sharing information gleaned during monitoring to improve services, such as solutions to common problems or promising practices. ORR and PRM officials identified some informal mechanisms for sharing such information with service providers, but relied mostly on service providers to network among themselves or share information during quarterly conference calls and annual consultations. ORR also relies on external technical assistance providers to disseminate best practices when training grantees and expects state refugee coordinators to share findings of monitoring reports with their local partners. However, monitoring reports are not publicly available, and, unless the state coordinators share this information, service providers may not be able to identify promising practices, track monitoring results, identify trends, and address common issues. As a result, service providers do not always get the information they need to improve services, whether by preventing a problem or implementing a best practice.

ORR's Performance Measures Encourage Service Providers to Focus on Short-Term Outcomes

ORR's performance measures focus on short-term outcomes, even though refugees remain eligible for social services funded by ORR for up to 5 years.[44] Because it is important for refugees to become employed before their cash assistance runs out—8 months or less, depending on the service delivery model—ORR's performance measures provide incentives for service providers to focus on helping refugees gain and maintain employment quickly. Specifically, ORR requires grantees to measure entered employment at 6 months for the Matching Grant program or 8 months for statewide cash assistance programs.[45] In addition, ORR requires grantees to measure job retention 90 days after employment. This focus on short-term employment, however, can result in a one-size-fits-all approach to employment services and may, in turn, limit service providers' flexibility to provide services that may benefit refugees after the 6 to 8 month time frame. That is, with limited incentives to focus on longer-term employment and wages, service providers may not help refugees obtain longer-term services and training, such as on-the-job or vocational training, which could significantly boost their income or benefit the refugee in the long-term or after employment is measured.[46] For example, when assisting refugees who arrive with college degrees and professional experience, service providers may not help them earn a credential valid in the United States, because the providers' effectiveness

---

[44] Employment is measured for all cash assistance recipients, but after cash assistance expires, employment is measured only for refugees who are enrolled in ORR-funded employment assistance. The portion of the caseload that is receiving employment services but not receiving cash assistance varies widely by state. For example, in 2010 in California, 12 percent of the caseload was not receiving federal cash assistance, but in Wisconsin, 66 percent of the caseload was receiving no federal cash assistance. ORR requires service providers to give newly arrived refugees priority for services. Some service providers have said that in order to ensure that new arrivals continued to receive needed services, they provided employment services to refugees for only about 1 year rather than the 5 years allowed.

[45] Our 2011 report provides more information about the various ways states may opt to deliver services. See GAO-11-369. All states, except Wyoming, administer an ORR-funded assistance program that provides up to 8 months of cash and medical assistance, as well as other social services. In addition, some refugees participate in the Matching Grant program, which is only partially funded by ORR. According to ORR, a network of national voluntary agencies administers this program. The Matching Grant program provides refugees with cash and other assistance for 4 to 6 months with the goal of helping them become self-sufficient without receiving cash benefits from a public assistance program.

[46] States do report to ORR the number of refugees they serve who have been in the United States for more than 12 months. ORR officials noted that refugees may also access mainstream employment services.

is measured by whether the refugee is employed. Additionally, ORR does not allow skills certification training to exceed 1 year and requires the refugees to be employed when receiving training and services.[47] Several service providers mentioned this as a challenge for highly skilled Iraqi refugees, in particular, some of whom include doctors and engineers.[48]

In addition, voluntary agency officials noted that ORR's employment measures do not allow them to report on the longer-term or non-employment-related outcomes of the other refugee resettlement services they provide. As a result, services such as skills training, English language training, or mental health services—which provide longer-term benefits and benefits unrelated to employment—may not be emphasized. According to some local voluntary agency officials we spoke to, given the current performance measures, there is a disincentive to dedicate necessary time and resources to the nonemployment activities that create pathways to success for refugees. It may be particularly difficult to serve those who do not arrive in the United States ready to work due to trauma, illness, or lack of basic skills.

While much of ORR's grant funding focuses on short-term employment, ORR does have some discretionary grants that provide funding for particular purposes that may include services that focus on longer-term goals or more intensive case management. For example, the individual development account program provides matching funds to help refugees save money for the purchase of a vehicle or a home.[49] For these

---

[47] Obtaining credentials may require additional training, including English language training, which may go beyond 6 or 8 months.

[48] A study commissioned by ORR on its social service and targeted assistance grant highlighted a career-laddering program in Miami as a promising practice. The purpose of the program is to help refugees who were professionals in their native countries but who lack certification to do similar work in the United States. The program helps refugees with obtaining credentials, training, and employment in a field that is consistent with their career goals and similar to the work they did in their native countries. HHS, *The Evaluation of the Refugee Social Service (RSS) and Targeted Assistance Formula Grant (TAG) Programs: Synthesis of Findings from Three Sites* (Washington, D.C.: March 2008). ORR also partially funds two other programs that promote professional recertification of refugee physicians and other highly skilled professionals. One is located in Minnesota. The other is located in San Diego, California.

[49] The individual development account program provides refugees with matched savings accounts for the purchase of specific assets: a home, capital for a small business, post-secondary education or training, and in some cases, the purchase of a car if needed to maintain or upgrade employment.

relatively small competitively awarded discretionary grant programs, ORR gathers data on how much money was saved and what assets were purchased, but does not gather data on how these asset purchases affected earnings or self-sufficiency. Descriptions of discretionary grants that can be used to fund services beyond the initial resettlement period, as well as other selected ORR and PRM grant programs, can be found in appendix IV.

In addition to the employment measures' focus on short term outcomes, one state coordinator also noted that these employment measures leave room for interpretation. Specifically, some voluntary agencies may have a narrow definition of employment services while others may have a broader definition. In turn, the percentage of refugees who become employed after receiving employment services could vary based on what types of services are considered employment services. As a result, according to a state coordinator, measures may not provide consistent information about how well a program is performing in different communities.

Little Is Known about the Extent of Refugee Integration, but Studies Offer a Framework for Assessing Integration

Federal Agencies Promote but Do Not Currently Measure Refugee Integration

While federal refugee resettlement programs generally provide only short-term assistance, PRM and ORR both aim to prepare refugees for long-term integration into their communities. Although there is no single, generally accepted definition of integration in the literature, integration can be defined as a dynamic, multidirectional process in which newcomers and the receiving communities intentionally work together, based on a shared commitment to acceptance and justice, to create a secure, welcoming, vibrant, and cohesive society.[50] The federal government's efforts to facilitate integration begin before refugees even enter the United States, as PRM offers cultural orientation for all refugees and recently piloted English language training for refugees in certain overseas locations.[51] According to PRM, this cultural orientation and language training is intended to lay the groundwork for refugees' long-term integration into the United States. Integration is also a part of ORR's mission and overall goal,[52] and officials told us that they consider integration to be a central aspect of refugee resettlement. Although ORR only provides refugees with cash and medical assistance for a maximum of 8 months, officials noted that this initial assistance helps set the foundation for long-term integration. Other ORR programs provide longer-term services that are intended to further facilitate integration, but these services may not be as widely available as cash and medical assistance. For example, ORR's social services grant program funds employment services and other support services to refugees for up to 5 years after arrival, but communities may choose to provide these services for a shorter period of time due to local resource constraints. ORR's discretionary grants for micro-enterprise assistance and individual development accounts are also designed to facilitate integration by helping refugees start businesses in the communities where they live, among other goals.[53] However, these discretionary grants are competitively awarded and are thus not available to all communities.

---

[50] This definition is the working definition adopted by ORR's integration working group, and is not an official definition adopted by ORR. ORR created an integration working group in 2006 to review and analyze the integration process for refugees in communities throughout the United States.

[51] PRM offers cultural orientation in both overseas locations and the resettlement location in the United States, and recently piloted English language training programs in Kenya, Thailand, and Nepal.

[52] ORR's mission statement is: "Founded on the belief that newly arriving populations have inherent capabilities when given opportunities, the Office of Refugee Resettlement (ORR) provides people in need with critical resources to assist them in becoming integrated members of American society." ORR's major goal is to "provide assistance to refugees and other eligible persons through its various programs and grants, so that they can achieve self-sufficiency and integration within the shortest time period after arriving in the United States."

[53] The micro-enterprise assistance program provides refugees with loans and training to start, expand, or strengthen their own businesses. As noted above, the individual development account program provides refugees with matched savings accounts for the purchase of specific assets, including capital for a small business.

ORR has studied approaches that facilitate refugee integration. In 2006, ORR created an integration working group to identify indicators of refugee integration and ways in which ORR could more fully support the integration process. In a 2007 interim report, the working group made both short-term and long-term recommendations to ORR, including that it (1) consider expanding ORR's discretionary grant programs; (2) focus on integration in the areas of employment, English language acquisition, health, housing, and civic engagement; and (3) identify lessons learned from communities where refugee integration appears to be taking place. ORR officials told us that they have implemented many, but not all, of the working group's recommendations due to funding constraints.[54] For example, ORR commissioned a study to identify promising practices that appear to facilitate integration in four U.S. cities.[55]

Neither PRM nor ORR currently measure refugee integration as a program outcome. According to PRM, it does not measure refugee integration due to the short-term nature of the Reception and Placement Program. While refugee integration is part of ORR's mission and overall goal, ORR officials said they have not measured it because there is no clear definition of integration, because it is unclear when integration should be measured, and because the Refugee Act focuses on self-sufficiency outcomes related to employment. Even so, ORR officials told us that they collect some data related to refugee integration. Specifically, as part of its annual report to Congress, ORR conducts a survey to gauge refugees' economic self-sufficiency that includes integration-related measures such as employment, English language proficiency, participation in job training, attendance in a high school or university degree or certificate program, and home ownership.[56] However, ORR officials noted that the survey is not designed to measure integration and should not be used for this purpose, especially since there is no clear

---

[54] See appendix V for a complete list of the working group's recommendations to ORR and their implementation status.

[55] ISED Solutions, *Exploring Refugee Integration: Experiences in Four American Communities*, a report prepared at the request of the Department of Health and Human Services Office of Refugee Resettlement (ORR), June 2010. We included this study in our literature review.

[56] Each year, an ORR contractor surveys a random sample of refugees selected from the population of all refugees who arrived in the U.S. in the last 5 years.

definition of integration. In addition, the survey has had a low response rate, which may affect the quality of the data.[57]

Studies Offer a Framework for Measuring and Facilitating Integration

Studies on refugee resettlement do not offer a broad assessment of how well refugees have integrated into the United States. Of the 13 studies we identified that addressed refugee integration, almost all were limited in scope in that they focused on particular refugee groups in specific geographic locations.[58] The studies describe the integration experiences of specific refugee groups, including factors that help refugees successfully integrate into their communities. However, because of the studies' limited scope and differences in their methodologies, they provide limited insight into how refugees overall have integrated in the United States or how the experiences of different groups compare to one another.

Although the studies we reviewed were not directly comparable, together they identified a variety of indicators that can be used to assess progress toward integration for both individuals and communities, as well as common facilitators of integration. Indicators of integration include employment, English language acquisition, housing, physical and mental health, and social connections, as well as political involvement, citizenship status, and participation in community organizations. One study noted that when assessing integration, it is important to ask refugees whether they consider themselves to be integrated.

The studies we reviewed also identified a range of barriers to integration. Some frequently cited barriers were a lack of formal education, illiteracy or limited English proficiency, and insufficient income from low-paying jobs. For example, refugees who are illiterate or have limited English proficiency may be limited to low-paying jobs such as hotel housekeepers and may not earn sufficient income to meet their needs. Furthermore, one study found that the timing of employment can be a barrier to integration. Specifically, the study found that taking a job soon after arrival can slow down the acquisition of English language skills because refugees may have less available time to attend language classes.

---

[57] For example, the survey response rate was 50.3 percent in 2008 and 36.6 percent in 2007.

[58] See appendix II for a list of the studies we included in our literature review.

In addition, the studies we reviewed identified facilitators of integration—circumstances and strategies that can help refugees integrate successfully into their communities. English language acquisition is an important facilitator of integration. For example, one study found that refugees who are proficient in English are better able to connect with nonrefugees in their communities, expanding their social connections and sources of support. Other facilitators of integration included employment, social support from other refugees, and affiliation with or sponsorship by a religious congregation. For example, religious congregations may provide refugees with language classes, social activities, emotional and financial support, and linkages with employment and educational opportunities, medical care, and transportation. See table 6 for additional examples of indicators of integration, barriers to integration, and facilitators of integration.

Table 6: Selected Integration Indicators, Barriers, and Facilitators Identified in Literature Review

Indicators of integration	Barriers to integration	Facilitators of integration
Civic participation	None identified	• Political involvement • Community organizing of refugee groups
Culture	• Unfamiliarity with "Western" culture • Intolerance for non-English speakers • Intolerance for cultural or religious differences	• Availability of public service providers to educate community about refugees' cultures (and vice versa)
Education or training	• Lack of or little formal education prior to arrival in the U.S. • Lack of options for re-credentialing for skilled workers or professionals	• Adult education opportunities
Employment	• Insufficient income from low-paying jobs • Workplace environments with no opportunity to speak English	• English proficiency, which may help refugees obtain work that generates sufficient income • Networks and support groups that help refugees find employment • Ethnic small businesses

Indicators of integration	Barriers to integration	Facilitators of integration
English language acquisition	• Illiteracy or limited English proficiency • "Work first" emphasis, which may slow language acquisition if it limits time to attend English classes	• Opportunities to learn and practice speaking English • Participation in English classes for an extended period of time
Host community	• Harassment and discrimination • Negative interactions with government entities, creating mistrust • Limited resources of agencies serving refugees	• Preparation of the community to receive newcomers • Bilingual and culturally competent staff at agencies serving refugees • Community events to celebrate refugees' cultures
Housing	• Inadequate housing • Low-income, high-crime neighborhoods • Housing settings with no opportunity to speak English	• Moving out of low-income neighborhoods
Social connections	• Social isolation	• Social support from other refugees • Friendship or mentoring programs • Community dinners and gardens • Affiliation with or sponsorship by a religious congregation

Source: GAO literature review.

Some Communities Have Developed Formal Plans for Refugee Integration

While most of the communities we visited had not established formal goals or strategies to facilitate refugee integration, two of the eight communities had developed formal plans to promote integration. The City of Boise, for example, developed a plan to facilitate the successful resettlement of refugees that includes goals related to integration. Specifically, the plan aims to facilitate integration by (1) establishing refugee community centers, (2) using a media campaign to increase community awareness and support of refugees, and (3) creating a mentoring program for refugee youth, among other things. Similarly, the Village of Skokie, Illinois, a suburb of Chicago, created a strategic plan to help facilitate the integration of immigrants, including refugees, by (1) establishing a coordinating council of key service providers, (2) developing a system to improve providers' access to interpreters, and (3) recruiting and training immigrant and refugee community leaders for government commissions and school boards, among other strategies.

Additionally, in Lancaster, Pennsylvania, Franklin & Marshall College had taken a variety of steps to help facilitate the integration of refugees, including using student volunteers to teach refugees English, tutor refugee students, and help refugee families enroll their children in school and access public health services. In addition, at the time of our visit, the college was partnering with a local voluntary agency affiliate to plan a community conference on refugee integration with the goals of (1) better understanding and addressing the needs of refugees, (2) identifying strategies for fostering rapid integration, and (3) developing a broad coalition of organizations serving refugees that could continue to work together on these issues in the future.

Conclusions

Each year, as part of its humanitarian role in the international community, the United States admits tens of thousands of refugees who add richness and diversity to our society but can also have a significant impact on the communities in which they live, particularly in cases where relevant state and local stakeholders are not consulted before refugees are resettled. Advance consultation is important because stakeholders need time to plan so that they can properly serve refugees when they arrive, and because their input on the number of refugees to be resettled can help communities avoid reaching a crisis point. Information about communities that have developed effective strategies for consultation would likely benefit other communities facing similar obstacles. Without more specific guidance and information on effective strategies for consultation, communities may continue to struggle to meet refugees' needs, which may negatively affect both refugees and their communities and would likely deter integration. Similarly, while ORR has recognized that some service providers have particularly effective strategies for resettlement, neither ORR nor PRM disseminate this information to other service providers. As a result, not all communities are aware of ways they can do their work more effectively.

Furthermore, while refugees can receive resettlement services for up to 5 years, some find it difficult to access those services when they relocate to another community. In addition, states do not receive increased funding for serving secondary migrants until the year after refugees relocate. As a result, in communities that experience high levels of secondary migration, voluntary agencies and service providers may not have the resources to provide services to the migrants who need them. Without a funding process that would respond more quickly to localities experiencing high rates of secondary migration, voluntary agencies may have to prioritize serving recently arrived refugees and communities may find their resources for refugees stretched too thin.

As required by the Immigration and Nationality Act, as amended, ORR's programs are designed to help refugees become employed as quickly as possible. ORR's measures of effectiveness, which focus on whether refugees gain employment in the short term, in turn, influence the types of services that refugees receive. Specifically, service providers may choose to provide services that encourage short-term independence from cash assistance, but might not help refugees achieve long-term self-sufficiency. However, refugees may face unique challenges such as a lack of formal education or work experience, language barriers, and physical and mental health conditions that can make the transition to the United States difficult. Without some incentives to focus on long-term self-sufficiency in addition to short-term independence from cash assistance, refugees may be more likely to need government assistance again in the future, and it may take longer for both refugees and their communities to experience the benefits of integration.

Recommendations for Executive Action

We are making the following four recommendations based on our review:

To help ensure that state and local stakeholders have the opportunity to provide input on the number of refugees resettled in their communities, we recommend that

- the Secretary of State provide additional guidance to resettlement agencies and state coordinators on how to consult with local stakeholders prior to making placement decisions, including with whom to consult and what should be discussed during the consultations; and
- the Secretaries of State and of Health and Human Services collect and disseminate best practices related to refugee placement decisions, specifically on working with community stakeholders, as well as other promising practices from communities.

To assist communities in providing services to secondary migrants, we recommend that the Secretary of Health and Human Services consider additional ways to increase the responsiveness of the grants designed for this purpose. This could include asking states to report secondary migration data more often than once a year, allowing resubmission of secondary migration data from states that was rejected because it did not match ORR's database, creating a process for counting migrants who received services in more than one state, and establishing an emergency grant that could be used to more quickly identify and assist communities that are struggling to serve high levels of secondary migrants.

To give service providers more flexibility to serve refugees with different needs and to create incentives to focus on longer term goals, including integration, independence from any government services, and career advancement, we recommend that the Secretary of Health and Human Services examine ORR's performance measures in light of its goals and determine whether changes are needed.

Agency Comments and Our Evaluation

We shared a draft of this report with HHS and State for review and comment. In its written comments, reproduced in appendix VI, HHS generally concurred with our recommendations. Specifically, HHS stated that it supports our recommendation to disseminate best practices, including promising practices from communities, while noting that State and nonprofit community-based and faith-based organizations have traditionally taken the lead on resettling refugees. HHS highlighted the efforts it has made in conducting quarterly placement meetings, which include resettlement agencies and refugee coordinators. While these meetings may be helpful, we believe that HHS can also implement this recommendation by disseminating best practices and program strengths that it documents through its monitoring of states and service providers.

In addition, HHS concurred with our recommendation that it consider additional ways to increase the responsiveness of grants that help communities provide services to secondary migrants, but noted that it already provides Supplemental Services grants, which provide short-term assistance to areas that are impacted by increased numbers of new arrivals or secondary migrants. In addition, it raised concerns that an increase in the frequency of data collection would significantly increase the reporting burden without a mandatory need for the data. HHS also stated that it has a process in place for notifying states of technical problems with population data submitted and allowing them to make corrections. While we recognize that HHS has strategies in place to serve secondary migrants, we continue to believe that (1) the Supplemental Services grants can be improved to be more responsive; (2) more up-to-date population data can help HHS respond more quickly to communities experiencing high levels of secondary migration; and (3) improvements can be made to the process for correcting population data.

HHS also stated that it will consider modifying its performance measures and will also continue to assess the usefulness of data elements collected through required reporting to ensure that the program addresses both self-sufficiency and integration. HHS noted, for example, that it has already begun collecting more information about health through its annual survey of refugees and expanded the number of reporting elements pertaining to health in its program performance reporting form. In addition, it is developing approaches to increase the overall participation rates in its annual survey.

In its written comments, reproduced in appendix VII, State generally concurred with our recommendations and outlined steps it will take to address them. HHS and State also provided technical comments that were incorporated, as appropriate.

As agreed with your offices, unless you publicly announce the contents of this report earlier, we plan no further distribution until 30 days from the report date. At that time, we will send copies to relevant congressional committees, the Secretary of Health and Human Services, the Secretary of State, and other interested parties. In addition, the report will be available at no charge on the GAO Web site at http://www.gao.gov.

If you or your staff have any questions about this report, please contact me at (202) 512-7215 or brownke@gao.gov. Contact points for our Offices of Congressional Relations and Public Affairs may be found on the last page of this report. Key contributors to this report are listed in appendix VIII.

Kay E. Brown

Kay E. Brown
Director, Education, Workforce, and Income Security Issues

List of Requesters

The Honorable Richard G. Lugar
Ranking Member
Committee on Foreign Relations
United States Senate

The Honorable Patrick Leahy
Chairman
Committee on the Judiciary
United States Senate

The Honorable Bob Corker
United States Senate

The Honorable Duncan Hunter
House of Representatives

The Honorable Gary C. Peters
House of Representatives

Appendix I: Objectives, Scope, and Methodology

To identify the factors resettlement agencies consider when deciding where refugees are initially placed, we reviewed relevant federal and state laws and regulations and other relevant documents, and conducted interviews with federal agency officials and national voluntary agency staff. We interviewed officials from the U.S. Department of State's Bureau of Population, Refugees, and Migration (PRM) and the Department of Health and Human Services' Office of Refugee Resettlement (ORR), as well as representatives from several national voluntary resettlement agencies. We also reviewed documents related to the refugee placement process, such as relevant federal and state laws and regulations, guidance for determining community capacity to resettle refugees, the terms of the cooperative agreements between PRM and national voluntary agencies, and funding opportunity announcements for PRM's Reception and Placement Program.

To understand the effects refugees have on their communities, we met with experts on refugee programs and conducted site visits to eight communities across the United States where we met with representatives from state and local government entities, voluntary agency affiliates, community-based organizations, local businesses, and other relevant individuals and groups, including refugees, professors from local universities, and a local church that provided assistance to refugees.[1] For our site visits, we selected Boise, Idaho; Chicago, Illinois; Detroit, Michigan; Fargo, North Dakota; Knoxville, Tennessee; Lancaster, Pennsylvania; Owensboro, Kentucky; and Seattle, Washington.[2] These eight communities represent a nongeneralizable sample that was selected to include geographically distributed communities with variations in their population sizes, levels of experience resettling refugees, and racial and ethnic diversity. In addition to these factors, several communities were selected because they are considered examples of best practices in refugee resettlement by federal officials. All of the selected communities were receiving refugees at the time we visited. We developed site selection criteria based on available literature that discussed factors that influence the impact of refugees on their respective communities and factors that either facilitate or hinder refugee integration.

---

[1] We did not meet with all of these groups in every community we visited.

[2] As part of our site visit to Chicago, we also met with city officials in Skokie, Illinois. Our visit to the Detroit area focused on the cities of Dearborn and Sterling Heights, Michigan. Our visit to Seattle included interviews with relevant groups in Kent, Washington.

We used these criteria in combination with one another to arrive at a
diverse set of communities with varying characteristics.

To assess the effectiveness and integrity of refugee resettlement
programs, we interviewed federal agency officials, state coordinators, and
local voluntary agencies. We also reviewed federal agencies' monitoring
plans, protocols and selected monitoring reports for the communities we
visited. We reviewed the terms of the cooperative agreements between
PRM and national voluntary agencies, as well as reporting guidance,
sample performance reports, and performance measures federal
agencies use to monitor their programs.

To determine what is known about refugees' integration into the United
States, we conducted a literature review of academic research on this
topic. To identify relevant studies, we conducted searches of various
databases including Academic OneFile, EconLit, Education Resources
Information Center, National Technical Information Service, PAIS
International, PASCAL, ProQuest, PsycINFO, Social Sciences Abstracts,
Social Services Abstracts, Social SciSearch, Sociological Abstracts, and
WorldCat. We conducted a search using the following criteria, which
yielded 18 studies:

- Studies must address the integration of refugees into U.S.
  communities; [3]
- Studies must have been published from 1995 to the present;
- Studies must be in English; and
- Studies must be scholarly, such as peer-reviewed journal articles.

We performed these searches and identified studies between August
2011 and October 2011.

In addition, ORR officials provided us with an ORR-commissioned study
of promising practices that appear to facilitate refugee integration, and
this study met our selection criteria.

To assess the methodological quality of the 18 studies that met our
selection criteria, we evaluated each study's research methodology,
including whether the study was original research, the reliability of the

---

[3] We excluded studies addressing refugees' integration into the countries where they first
sought asylum.

data set, if applicable, and the study's findings, assumptions, and
limitations. We determined that 13 of the 18 studies were sufficiently
reliable for our purposes. We then analyzed the findings of these 13
studies.[4]

In addition to conducting a literature review, we met with officials from
ORR and PRM to determine what, if any, efforts the federal government
has to define, measure, or facilitate refugees' integration into the United
States. We discussed refugee integration in our interviews with state and
local entities during our site visits. We also reviewed the ORR integration
working group's 2007 interim report and ORR's annual reports to
Congress.

We also obtained secondary migration data from ORR's annual report.
We assessed the reliability of this data by interviewing ORR officials
knowledgeable about the data. We determined that the data were
sufficiently reliable for the purpose of background in this report.

We conducted this performance audit from May 2011 through July 2012
in accordance with generally accepted government auditing standards.
Those standards require that we plan and perform the audit to obtain
sufficient, appropriate evidence to provide a reasonable basis for our
findings and conclusions based on our audit objectives. We believe that
the evidence obtained provides a reasonable basis for our findings and
conclusions based on our audit objectives.

---

[4] See appendix II for a list of the studies we included in our literature review.

Appendix II: Studies Included in Literature Review

Abu-Ghazaleh, F. "Immigrant Integration in Rural Communities: The Case of Morgan County." *National Civic Review*, vol. 98, no. 1 (2009).

Birman, D., and N. Tran. "Psychological Distress and Adjustment of Vietnamese Refugees in the United States: Association with Pre- and Postmigration Factors." *American Journal of Orthopsychiatry*, vol. 78, no. 1 (2008).

Duchon, D. A. "Home Is Where You Make It: Hmong Refugees in Georgia." *Urban Anthropology*, vol. 26, no. 1 (1997).

Franz, B. "Transplanted or Uprooted? Integration Efforts of Bosnian Refugees Based Upon Gender, Class and Ethnic Differences in New York City and Vienna." *The European Journal of Women's Studies*, vol. 10, no. 2 (2003).

Grigoleit, G. "Coming Home? The Integration of Hmong Refugees from Wat Tham Krabok, Thailand, into American Society." *Hmong Studies Journal*, vol. 7 (2006).

Hume, S.E., and S.W. Hardwick. "African, Russian, and Ukrainian Refugee Resettlement in Portland, Oregon." *The Geographical Review*, vol. 95, no. 2 (2005).

ISED Solutions. Exploring Refugee Integration: Experiences in Four American Communities. A report prepared at the request of the Department of Health and Human Services Office of Refugee Resettlement. June 2010.

Ives, N. "More than a 'Good Back': Looking for Integration in Refugee Resettlement." *Refuge*, vol. 24, no. 2 (2007).

Kenny, P., and K. Lockwood-Kenny. "A Mixed Blessing: Karen Resettlement to the United States." *Journal of Refugee Studies*, vol. 24, no. 2 (2011).

Patil, C.L., M. McGown, P.D. Nahayo, and C. Hadley. "Forced Migration: Complexities in Food and Health for Refugees Resettled in the United States." *NAPA Bulletin*, vol. 34, issue 1 (2010).

Shandy, D., and K. Fennelly. "A Comparison of the Integration
Experiences of Two African Immigrant Populations in a Rural
Community." *Journal of Religion & Spirituality in Social Work*, vol. 25, no.
1 (2006).

Smith, R.S. "The Case of a City Where 1 in 6 Residents is a Refugee:
Ecological Factors and Host Community Adaptation in Successful
Resettlement." *American Journal of Community Psychology*, vol. 42, no.
3-4 (2008).

Westermeyer, J.J. "Refugee Resettlement to the United States:
Recommendations for a New Approach." *The Journal of Nervous and
Mental Disease*, vol. 199, no. 8 (2011).

Appendix III: 20 States with Largest Numbers of Refugees Arriving in FY 2011 and Refugees' Countries of Origin

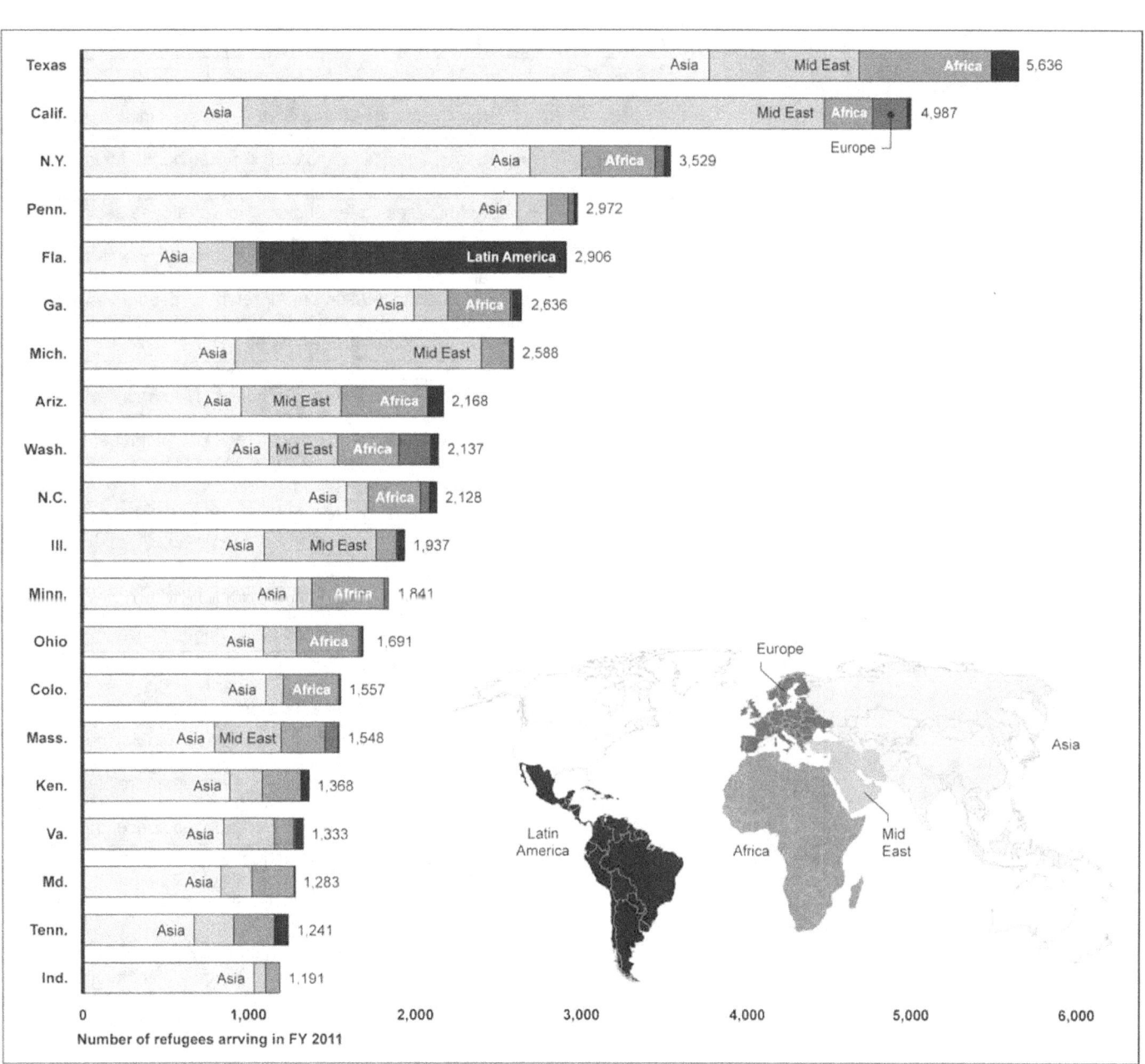

Source: GAO analysis of data from Department of State Refugee Processing Center; National Atlas (world map).

GAO-12-729 Refugee Resettlement

Appendix IV: Selected PRM and ORR Grant Programs

Agency	Grant	Type	Recipient	Description
PRM	Reception and Placement	Cooperative agreement	National Voluntary Agencies	Provides financial support to partially cover resettlement services based on a fixed per capita sum per refugee resettled in the United States. Services include arranging for refugees' placement and providing refugees with basic necessities and core services during their initial resettlement period.
ORR	Refugee Cash and Medical Assistance	Formula	States[a]	Reimburses states and alternative refugee assistance programs for the cost of cash and medical assistance provided to refugees[b] during the first 8 months after their arrival in this country or grant of asylum. It does not provide reimbursement for refugees deemed eligible for Temporary Assistance for Needy Families, Supplemental Security Insurance, and Medicaid.
	Voluntary Agency Matching Grant	Cooperative agreement	National Voluntary Agencies	Funds are provided on a matching basis to provide private, nonprofit organizations to fund an alternative to public cash assistance and to support case management, employment services, maintenance assistance, cash allowance, and social services for new arrivals for 4 to 6 months.
	Refugee Social Services	Formula	States	Provides funding for employment and other social services to refugees for 5 years after their data of arrival or grant of asylum.
	Targeted Assistance Grant	Formula	States	Provides funding for employment-related and other social services for refugees in counties with large refugee populations and high refugee concentrations.
	Preventative Health	Discretionary	States and designated health agencies	Provides funds to provide medical screenings to newly arriving refugees, interpreter services, information and referral, and health education.
	Targeted Assistance Discretionary	Discretionary	States	Funds to states to implement special employment services not implemented with formula social services grants. Provides funding for employment-related and other social services for refugees in counties with large refugee populations and high refugee concentrations.
	School Impact	Discretionary	States	Provides funds to subcontract with local school systems and nonprofits to support local school systems that are impacted by significant numbers of newly arrived refugee children.
	Services to Older Refugees	Discretionary	States	Provide funds to ensure that older refugees will be linked to mainstream aging services in their communities or to provide services directly to older refugees if they are not currently being provided for in the community.

Agency	Grant	Type	Recipient	Description
	Preferred Communities Program	Discretionary	National voluntary agencies	The Preferred Communities Program supports the resettlement of newly arriving refugees with the best opportunities for their self-sufficiency and integration into new communities, and supports refugees with special needs that require more intensive case management, culturally and linguistically appropriate linkages and coordination with other service providers to improve their access to services.
	Services for Survivors of Torture	Discretionary	Nonprofit organizations, voluntary agencies, local governments	Provides funding for a comprehensive program of support for survivors of torture, including rehabilitation, social and legal services, and training for providers.
	Individual Development Account	Discretionary	Nonprofit organizations, voluntary agencies, state and local governments	Funds projects to establish and manage Individual Development Accounts, which are matched savings accounts available for the purchase of specific assets. Matching funds, together with the refugee's own savings, are available for purchasing one (or more) of four savings goals: home purchase; microenterprise capitalization; postsecondary education or training; and purchase of an automobile if necessary for employment or educational purposes.
	Technical Assistance	Discretionary— Cooperative agreement	Nonprofit organizations, voluntary agencies	Grants to enable organizations with expertise in a particular area to provide assistance to ORR-funded agencies.
	Microenterprise Development	Discretionary	Nonprofit organizations, voluntary agencies, state and local governments	Provides funding to assist refugees to become financially independent by helping them develop capital resources and business expertise to start, expand, or strengthen their own businesses. Microenterprise projects typically include components of training and technical assistance in business skills and business management, credit assistance, and credit in the form of micro loans.
	Refugee Agricultural Partnership	Discretionary	Nonprofit organizations, voluntary agencies, state and local governments	Provides agricultural and food related resources and technical information to refugee families that are consistent with their agrarian backgrounds, and results in rural and urban farming projects that supports increased incomes, access to quality and familiar foods, better physical and mental health, and integration into this society.
	Supplemental Services for Recently Arrived Refugees	Discretionary	Nonprofit organizations, voluntary agencies, state and local governments	Provides funds to provide services to newly arriving refugees or sudden and unexpected large secondary migration of refugees where communities are not sufficiently prepared in terms of linguistic or culturally appropriate services and/or do not have sufficient service capacity.
	Ethnic Community Self-Help	Discretionary	Nonprofit organizations	Provides funds to support ethnic community based organizations in providing refugee populations with critical services to assist them in becoming integrated members of American society.

Sources: ORR annual report, ORR grant announcements, ORR program descriptions, the Catalog of Federal Domestic Assistance, and PRM grant announcements. ORR also funds additional programs for certain populations, including the Cuban Haitian Program, Anti-Trafficking in Persons Program, and an Unaccompanied Alien Children Program.

[a]For the purposes of this table, states refers to state agencies, state alternative programs, and state replacement designees. State alternative programs include (1) the Wilson/Fish program, which gives states flexibility in how they provide assistance to refugees, including whether to administer assistance primarily through local voluntary agencies, and (2) the Public Private Partnership program, which allows states to partner with local voluntary agencies to provide assistance. State replacement designees are authorized by ORR to administer assistance to refugees when a state withdraws from all or part of the refugee program.

[b]For the purposes of this table, refugees refers to refugees, certain Amerasians from Viet Nam, Cuban and Haitian entrants, asylees, victims of a severe form of trafficking, and Iraqi and Afghan Special Immigrants.

Appendix V: Status of Integration Working Group's Recommendations to ORR

In January 2007, ORR's Integration Working Group made short-term and long-term recommendations regarding ways in which ORR could more fully support the integration process for refugees.

	Implemented	In process	Not implemented
Short-term recommendations			
Include integration language in all grant announcements.	X		
Review discretionary grant programs offered in the standing announcement, ensuring that they promote integration.	X		
Establish the Department of Health and Human Services as the lead federal agency for integration.			X
Consider expanding ORR's discretionary programs.			X
Focus on integration in the areas of employment, English language acquisition, health, housing, and civic engagement.	X		
Focus technical assistance providers to support integration as an intentional process leading to civic engagement and citizenship.	X		
Seek and fund pilot programs such as the Building the New American Community project.			X
Develop an initiative to support professional recertification and credentialing for qualified individuals.		X	
Long-term recommendations			
Identify and share best practices through a survey of states, mutual aid associations, and voluntary agencies.	X		
Identify lessons learned, including case studies, from communities in which integration appears to be working well and where there are challenges.	X		
Study the effect of ORR policy and funding initiatives to promote integration over a three to five year period.			X
Refine/develop/disseminate an action model to be used for other immigrants and marginalized populations.			X
Seek broader collaboration with nonfederal entities such as private foundations, businesses, financial institutions, and the United Way.	X		

Sources: Report of the Integration Working Group, January 2007, and information provided by ORR.

Appendix VI: Comments from the Department of Health and Human Services

DEPARTMENT OF HEALTH & HUMAN SERVICES   OFFICE OF THE SECRETARY

Assistant Secretary for Legislation
Washington, DC 20201

'JUL 1 3 2012

Kay E. Brown, Director
Education, Workforce, and Income Security Issues
U.S. Government Accountability Office
441 G Street NW
Washington, DC 20548

Dear Ms. Brown:

Attached are comments on the U.S. Government Accountability Office's (GAO) report entitled:
"REFUGEE RESETTLEMENT: Greater Consultation with Community Stakeholders Could
Strengthen Program" (GAO-12-729).

The Department appreciates the opportunity to review this report prior to publication.

Sincerely,

Jim R. Esquea
Assistant Secretary for Legislation

Attachment

**GENERAL COMMENTS OF THE DEPARTMENT OF HEALTH AND HUMAN
SERVICES (HHS) ON THE GOVERNMENT ACCOUNTABILITY OFFICE'S (GAO)
DRAFT REPORT ENTITLED, "REFUGEE RESETTLEMENT: GREATER
CONSULTATION WITH COMMUNITY STAKEHOLDERS COULD STRENGTHEN
PROGRAM" (GAO-12-729)**

The Department appreciates the opportunity to review and comment on this draft report. The draft report examines the factors resettlement agencies consider when determining where refugees are initially placed; the effects refugees have on their communities; how federal agencies ensure the effectiveness and integrity of refugee resettlement programs; and what is known about refugees' integration into the United States.

GAO Recommendation

The Secretaries of State and of Health and Human Services collect and disseminate best practices related to refugee placement decisions, specifically on working with community stakeholders, as well as other promising practices from communities.

HHS Comments

HHS recognizes that many factors should be considered when determining where refugees are initially placed and supports GAO's recommendation to collect and disseminate best practices on working with community stakeholders as well as other promising practices. The Department of State (DOS)/Bureau of Population, Refugees, and Migration (PRM), in collaboration with resettlement agencies, determines the placement of refugees. Although HHS's Administration for Children and Families' (ACF) Office of Refugee Resettlement (ORR) does not have a direct role in placement decisions, based on a directive from the White House, PRM and ORR conduct quarterly placement meetings that include resettlement agencies, State Refugee Coordinators, Refugee Health Coordinators, ORR funded technical assistance providers, and Ethnic Community Based Organizations. To date, ORR and PRM have jointly conducted five quarterly placement meetings providing program updates, data and other relevant information. ORR also provides DOS/PRM with major resettlement indicators, and supporting data and information, for consideration in their annual refugee allocation and placement decisions.

Historically, non-profit community-based and faith-based organizations have taken the lead in resettling refugees in the U.S. These organizations have insight into their respective local communities and can establish partnerships with hospitals, school districts, employers and business start-ups to create a win-win situation for refugees and local communities. As noted in the GAO report, refugee students can help stabilize the public school population and the refugee workforce can revitalize local economies by creating new businesses and jobs. HHS believes that a carefully coordinated approach to initial placement can lead to more successes like these and build upon on the positive effect that refugees have on local communities.

1

GENERAL COMMENTS OF THE DEPARTMENT OF HEALTH AND HUMAN SERVICES (HHS) ON THE GOVERNMENT ACCOUNTABILITY OFFICE'S (GAO) DRAFT REPORT ENTITLED, "REFUGEE RESETTLEMENT: GREATER CONSULTATION WITH COMMUNITY STAKEHOLDERS COULD STRENGTHEN PROGRAM" (GAO-12-729)

GAO Recommendation

To assist communities in providing services to secondary migrants, we recommend that the Secretary of Health and Human Services consider additional ways to increase the responsiveness of the grants designed for this purpose. This could include asking states to report secondary migration data more often than once a year, or allowing resubmission of rejected reimbursement claims from states; and establishing an emergency grant that could be used to more quickly identify and assist communities that are struggling to serve high levels of secondary migrants.

HHS Comments

HHS concurs with the GAO recommendation to consider ways to increase the responsiveness of grants to areas impacted by secondary migration. In addition to the Social Services formula grants, which are adjusted each year by factors such as secondary migration, ACF also implements the Supplemental Services program. The purpose of the program is to provide short-term assistance – 17 months – to bridge funding availability in areas that are impacted by increased new arrivals or secondary migrants until the following year's Social Services formula allocation. ORR has also sent teams of ORR staff and technical assistance providers to areas impacted by large numbers of new arrivals or secondary migrants to provide assistance and guidance to service providers. ORR will continue to consider these and other options to provide rapid assistance to impacted areas.

GAO also recommends changes in grantee reporting on the eligible population. Currently ORR collects data from states on secondary migration once a year in order to use the data for allocation of the Social Services formula grants and for the Annual Report to Congress. These allocations are based on the statutory requirement that the eligible population, including secondary migrants, as of September 30 of the preceding fiscal year, be used to determine the allocations.

GAO further recommends that the secondary migration data be collected more frequently and that resubmission of rejected reimbursement claims be allowed. HHS will consider this recommendation; however, we are concerned that an increase in data collection frequency would significantly increase the reporting burden for states without a mandatory need for the data.

With regard to the recommendation allowing resubmission of reimbursement claims, HHS assumes that this recommendation refers to submission of population data by states for use in the Social Services formula allocation. Currently, states are notified immediately of any technical problems with the data files that they submit and are given adequate time to make corrections.

2

**GENERAL COMMENTS OF THE DEPARTMENT OF HEALTH AND HUMAN
SERVICES (HHS) ON THE GOVERNMENT ACCOUNTABILITY OFFICE'S (GAO)
DRAFT REPORT ENTITLED, "REFUGEE RESETTLEMENT: GREATER
CONSULTATION WITH COMMUNITY STAKEHOLDERS COULD STRENGTHEN
PROGRAM" (GAO-12-729)**

GAO Recommendation

To give service providers more flexibility to serve refugees with different needs and to create
incentives to focus on longer term goals, including integration, independence from any
government services, and career advancement, we recommend that the Secretary of Health and
Human Services examine ORR's performance measures in light of its goals and determine
whether changes are needed.

HHS Comments

Currently, the performance measures for the U.S. domestic refugee resettlement program are
based on the Government Performance Results Act of 1993 and the self-sufficiency mandate
established in the Refugee Act of 1980. These measures focus on employability outcomes for all
refugees who receive employment services through the refugee resettlement program. This pool
of program participants includes refugees on short-term cash assistance (i.e., eight months of
Refugee Cash Assistance or longer-term Temporary Assistance for Needy Families) as well as
refugees who are not receiving any cash assistance and have lived in the U.S. for up to five
years. While self-sufficiency outcomes are central to this program, other outcomes, such as
health, support both the self-sufficiency and integration objectives of successful resettlement. In
the most recent revision of the program performance reporting form, ORR expanded the number
of data elements pertaining to health. ORR has also expanded the number of data elements being
collected through its annual survey of refugees and is developing approaches to increasing
overall participation rates in the survey. Finally, ORR recently established the Division of
Refugee Health and identified health and mental health services as one of the program's six
guiding principles[1]. ORR will continue to assess the usefulness of data elements collected
through its required reporting to ensure that the program addresses both self-sufficiency and
integration and we will explore considerations around modifying the measures.

---

[1] See State Letter 12-02, *Reorganization of Office of Refugee Resettlement* and 10-09, *Office of Refugee Resettlement Guiding
Principles* for more information.

3

Appendix VII: Comments from the Department of State

United States Department of State
Comptroller
1969 Dyess Avenue
Charleston, SC 29405

JUL 03 2012

Dr. Loren Yager
Managing Director
International Affairs and Trade
Government Accountability Office
441 G Street, N.W.
Washington, D.C. 20548-0001

Dear Dr. Yager:

We appreciate the opportunity to review your draft report, "REFUGEE RESETTLEMENT: Greater Consultation with Community Stakeholders Could Strengthen Program" GAO Job Code 131095.

The enclosed Department of State comments are provided for incorporation with this letter as an appendix to the final report.

If you have any questions concerning this response, please contact Barbara Day, Domestic Resettlement Section Chief, Bureau of Population, Refugees and Migration at (202) 453-9261.

Sincerely,

James L. Millette

cc: GAO – Kay Brown
      PRM– Anne Richard
      State/OIG – Evelyn Klemstine

Department of State Comments on GAO Draft Report

<u>**REFUGEE RESETTLEMENT: Greater Consultation with Community
Stakeholders Could Strengthen Program**</u>
(GAO-12-729, GAO Code 131095)

Thank you for the opportunity to comment on your draft report entitled, *"Refugee
Resettlement: Greater Consultation with Community Stakeholders Could
Strengthen Program."*

The Department of State accepts GAO's recommendation to provide additional
guidance to resettlement agencies and state coordinators for consultations with
local stakeholders before making placement decisions. We agree with GAO's
assessment that advance consultation gives stakeholders more time to plan so they
can better help refugees resettle. New guidance will include the range of
stakeholders to engage, topics to discuss, and requirements for reporting the
outcome of consultations. We will develop and evaluate this additional guidance
in collaboration with resettlement agencies and with input from state refugee
coordinators, state refugee health coordinators, state and local governments, and
local service providers.

The Department of State also accepts GAO's recommendation to collect and
disseminate best practices related to refugee placement decisions, specifically on
working with community stakeholders. We concur that sharing best practices likely
would benefit other communities facing similar situations. We will develop and
implement a mechanism for collecting and sharing those practices, with special
attention on the role stakeholders play in successful resettlement.

Finally, the Department of State acknowledges GAO's description of the bureau of
Population, Refugees and Migration's (PRM) time-limited responsibility to help
refugees integrate into their new communities and to assess the effectiveness of our
programs. We also acknowledge that the Office of Refugee Resettlement (ORR)
has primary responsibility for refugee integration following the brief reception and
placement period. We will consult with ORR to better coordinate our efforts to
promote integration and to develop meaningful performance measures of program
outcomes.

Appendix VIII: GAO Contacts and Staff Acknowledgments

GAO Contact	Kay E. Brown (202) 512-7215 or brownke@gao.gov
Staff Acknowledgments	In addition to the contact named above, Kathryn Larin, Assistant Director; Cheri Harrington and Lara Laufer, Analysts-in-Charge; James Bennett; David Chrisinger; Caitlin Croake; Bonnie Doty; Ashley McCall; Jean McSween; James Rebbe; and Carla Rojas made key contributions to this report. Sharon Hermes, Margaret Weber, and Amber Yancey Carroll verified our findings.

www.ingramcontent.com/pod-product-compliance
Lightning Source LLC
Chambersburg PA
CBHW080904290526
45795CB00007BA/2400